To Sandy & all her Hoeho

All our Love

Mickey & Semah

200 HOUSE PLANTS IN COLOR

200 HOUSE PLANTS IN COLOR

G. KROMDIJK

Translated by A. M. H. Speller

HERDER AND HERDER

1972
HERDER AND HERDER NEW YORK
1221 Avenue of the Americas, New York 10020

The plants shown in this book were collected and grown by Jet Kuyvenhoven and C. Bresser of Wageningen, Holland, and other amateurs whom the author and publisher wish to thank. Color photographs are by Rein Heij of Wageningen.

ISBN 07-07 3280-9
Library of Congress Catalog Card Number: 74-167 872
© 1967 by Zomer & Keuning, Wageningen
English translation © 1968 by Lutterworth Press
Printed in the Netherlands

Contents

Introduction   7

Hints for the care and cultivation of house plants   9
Light   9
Air   10
Water   10
Temperature   10
Feeding   11
Resting periods   11
Types of soil   11
Potting and re-potting of house plants   12
Pruning of plants   12
Aphids   12
House plants from seed   12
Taking cuttings of house plants   12
House plants in the garden   13
Dividing   13
Layering   13
Miniature greenhouse   13
House plants in bowls   14

Index   217

Introduction

When the publishers suggested preparing a book on house plants, based on colour pictures of as many as 200 plants with a description of each plant and its care, my reaction was: "What an ideal approach!". I was, of course, delighted to assist in its preparation and now that the book has been completed I feel that the original goal has been reached. In future if you are given a beautiful plant by a friend you will not have to worry about its correct name or how to look after it. A quick search through the exquisite colour photographs will identify the plant and instructions for its care are given below the picture. In giving these instructions as clearly and effectively as possible I have been helped by many questions which I have received from amateurs, as they enabled me to appreciate the most important of the difficulties which amateurs encounter. I hope the book will help to find a solution for the problems which are worrying them.

Early in the book the reader will find general hints on watering and manuring, seed-sowing, making cuttings and the requirements for light, air and correct temperature. This is followed by information concerning bowls of plants and miniature hothouses for indoor plants.

Finally, there is at the end of the book an index, which includes English and Latin names which should be of assistance.

The Dutch love for house plants is well known, and I hope that the English version of this book will contribute as much to the success of growing house plants as its original did in Holland.

When this book appeared in 1967 I could hardly expect that the interest in it would be so overwhelming. Reprint after reprint has appeared, and editions in Denmark, Britain, Finland, France, Germany, Jugoslavia, Norway, Spain and Sweden have appeared or will appear shortly. The total world edition five years after publication is already 450,000 copies. Also in this respect may our country as a country of flowers speak its word far beyond our borders. I am grateful to the publishers that they want to keep the book fully up-to-date. One new plant was added and twelve photographs of other plants have been renewed. Furthermore the names of the plants have been brought into agreement with the latest data, so that amateurs of plants will be kept properly informed as much as possible.

G. Kromdijk

Hints for the care and cultivation of house plants

It is not easy to define a house plant. No plants exist which will only grow indoors, but there are quite a large number of plants which are suitable for growing as house plants. Some can be grown indoors for a long time while others will survive for only a few weeks. Generally speaking, plants which attract attention because of their beautiful flowers or attractively shaped or coloured leaves, are chosen for growing as house plants. Whether or not a plant can be grown successfully indoors depends not only on where it is placed in the house, but also how it is treated. When keeping plants never forget that you are dealing with living things, and do not deprive them of your care for a single day. This does not mean that they should be watered every day, but a quick check should be made daily to see whether they need water or liquid manure.

In your absence they still need care and attention and they should not be left in an empty house. There is always a neighbour or friend to whom you can give the key of the house and who will look after your plants while you are away. If this is impossible, take them to somebody to look after or even, during the summer months, plunge them in their pots in the soil in the garden.

Before buying a plant, decide where you are going to keep it. There are various points to consider; two of the most important are light and atmosphere. Practically every house plant needs light. This does not mean that they should be placed in the full sun, because in some cases this could harm them. I often see plants tucked away in some dark corner or other. They are bound to fail unless a small light is placed above them during daytime (for this purpose a 20 watt lamp is sufficient). Many older houses are dark; in new houses the architect has usually planned for light and space and there one finds wide window ledges. These are ideal places for house plants. If the room faces South, it may become too hot during the day but this problem can be solved by having net curtains between the plants and the glass.

Atmosphere is of the greatest importance in the growing of plants. Just under two pints of water can be lost from the air in a heated room in a day, and this should be replaced for the sake of your plants as well as yourself.

Plants need not necessarily be confined to the living room. They can also be grown in other rooms, such as adjoining rooms, warmed by the fire in the main room. A plant in a bedroom looks pleasant, but do not have too many even though a few plants will not harm you.

Light Light is essential for most plants. If house plants were growing outside they would obviously have more light than is available in most situations inside a house. If you have a difficult plant which requires a lot of light you may have to give it artificial light during the day. Many kinds of plants can be cultivated on window ledges facing North, such as the miniature evergreen spruce, many fern varieties, also flowering Hydrangeas, Primulas in full flower, Begonia rex varieties, Aucuba Tradescantia and varieties of Palm.

Strong sunlight is suitable for most cacti and succulents, but leaf cactus, Zygocactus for example, prefers less sun. The morning sun is excellent for many plants.

Air As I mentioned earlier plants are living things, a fact which is not always remembered. They need air – preferably fresh air. In a room where people eat or smoke a great deal, you must provide a change of air at night, not only for yourself but also for the plants. Take care, if you open the window for a while, that your plants are not caught in a draught.

Water Watering is important in the cultivation of house plants and many mistakes are made since people seem to either over or under-water. I am often asked how much water a certain plant requires. This is a difficult question to answer; an Azalea should perhaps be watered once daily, a Hydrangea several times, a Begonia several times a week. A hanging Bellflower grown in a North aspect should be watered only once daily but the same plant grown in a window facing South should be watered several times a day. It is also important to remember when a plant's resting and growing periods are. A Bellflower which is watered twice a day during the summer needs hardly any water in the winter when it is resting. Cacti and succulents should also not be watered during their winter resting period although they can be given a lot of water in the summer months. Flowering plants such as Cyclamen, Primulas, Hydrangeas, Azaleas and Cinerarias require plenty of water during the winter and if in a warm room they need watering at least once a day. Remember never to use cold water, particularly for plants in an unheated room. Many people place their plants in saucers filled with water which is then taken up by the plants. If excessive water is removed after half an hour, this method is not harmful, although I prefer to water the soil from above. Very dry plants can be placed for a quarter of an hour to soak in a bucket of water with the pot immersed. Leave the plant a little longer if air-bubbles continue to rise, after which the soil should have become saturated.

The water you use should be slightly warm, especially when the plants are in a cool room. Warm water quickly cools and will not harm the roots.

It is important to syringe your plants as well as watering them, particularly if the atmosphere in a room is dry. Plants can be syringed until they are in full bud, but they should not be syringed when the plant is in flower. The immediate atmosphere around plants can also be made more humid by taking a deep, wide dish and placing an upturned saucer in the middle. The top of the saucer should be just above the water and the plant placed on top of it. There are now many plastic or decorative pots available which have a rim round the bottom in which water can be poured. This is yet another means of increasing the humidity round it.

How do you assess the humidity of a room? Well, if your husband's cigarettes should be damp, that is a better sign than if they are dry . . . that is, for your plants! You had better ask your husband whether his cigarettes are damp, and act accordingly.

Temperature Most plants prefer a moderate temperature (between 50° and 65° F.). If the temperature is too high for a certain plant in a heated room, then place it in the coolest place you have: for example in front of the window. This is also one of the best places for flowering plants and you will enjoy the blooms for the longest possible time. Bulbous plants in flower should not be placed in too warm a spot. Do not forget that plants in front of the window may easily freeze during wintertime. There is no danger of this in a normally heated room when there are only a few degrees of frost, but take care in unheated rooms and if necessary put newspapers in front of the window. If, in spite of these precautions your plants still freeze, or are in the least damaged by the frost, do not touch the flowers or leaves and do not place the pots in a warm room. It is much better to keep them for a few days in a cool but frost free cellar. Syringe them with cold water, direct from the tap. After a few days you will find out if they are going to revive or not.

You cannot subject tropical plants to such treatment as they definitely require a constant temperature of approximately 65° F. Often radiators are placed right underneath window sills, so please do not forget in such dry places to use the deep dish treatment with water to raise the humidity of the atmosphere. Electric and gas heating are both drying and you must bear this in mind.

Feeding   Plants need nourishment. Although this is normally present in the soil, it does not mean that there is always a sufficiency. The nurseryman supplies in the first instance nutritious potting compost but plants may have been in it for some time. Much of the goodness has been consumed and regular additional feeding has to be given. Most growing plants can be fed once or twice a week with liquid manure. It is better to give them a weak solution of liquid manure once a week rather than a strong solution every other week. Only plants in full growth require liquid manure while plants in their resting period should not be fed. How much liquid house plant manure should be given? A teaspoonful diluted in two pints of water is sufficient to treat approximately twenty plants. Ordinary manure, even well rotted cow-manure, is excellent but rarely available nowadays. Artificial manure for house plants can be obtained in various forms but it is better to stick to recognised brands.

Resting periods   You must not forget that the ancestors of our house plants were wild. Many plants grow in the wild in regions where there is no rainfall during certain periods of the year. They have adopted different methods of coping with this; some plants have prickles instead of leaves; others have leathery leaves or a kind of felt covering to reduce evaporation. Bromeliads, for example, have adopted in some instances tubular leaves which collect water, on which they exist during the dry periods. However well protected a plant may be against the dry season, it may not be sufficient, and for this reason many plants rest during a dry period. They then require less water in cultivation and should be given no liquid manure. We shall explain this in more detail when dealing with the individual plants.

Types of soil   If plants are to grow well in pots different types of soil are required for different kinds of plants. Fortunately one can buy excellent specially prepared mixtures of soil at a good nursery. There are even soils for Anthuriums and orchids so it is not necessary to make up your own mixtures. However, if you have your own garden you may wish to do so. Make a compost heap which should be turned over every three months. When this is well rotted it is the basis for an excellent potting compost. Sharp sand is added to this and if you can get it well rotted cow-manure. Some plants also require clay and this can conveniently be obtained from mole-hills on clay soil. Peat-moss can also be added to the compost and it is a necessity for Begonias and many tropical plants. Some plants also require Osmunda fibre and peat-moss in the compost but these can be obtained from the nursery.

Potting and re-potting of house plants   Do not forget that the cultivation of plants in pots is artificial although an art. In nature plants will grow in the open ground. The choice of pots for growing the plants in is easy. The best pots are ordinary earthenware ones which were usually used by nurserymen, but nowadays there are plastic pots which are cheap and plants usually like them. Please do not use glazed pots to grow plants in.
Decorative outer containers may be used but plants must still be kept in their ordinary earthenware pots. Soak new earthenware pots for a quarter of an hour in water before using them so that they become saturated.
You may ask should a plant be re-potted every spring? This is recommended, because it gives you the opportunity to remove the old spent soil and to replace it with fresh soil. Place a crock over the hole at the bottom of the pot to prevent it from becoming blocked up. A crock is generally a piece of a broken pot and therefore not flat. It prevents the soil from blocking the drainage hole at the base of the pot, but allows excessive moisture to drain away. You can say that potting differs from re-potting in that it is concerned with small cuttings or seedlings. Do not overpot. Later, when the plants have grown sufficiently, they can then be potted on into larger pots.

Pruning of plants   In the early spring many plants need cutting back and shaping. You will find details about this under each individual plant. Some plants have to be cut back, otherwise they grow straggly and thin. When there are new growths some 4 inches long, you can nip out the top, after which the plant will spread nicely.

Aphids   Aphids attack many varieties of plants and damage them considerably. There are many insecticides on sale. Please take note of the instructions on the container and if you follow them carefully you will be quite safe. After use, store the insecticide very carefully and out the reach of children as it may be poisonous. If the label comes off, stick a piece of paper on the container with the name on it, this will avoid accidents.

House plants from seed   House plants can be propagated from seeds. If this is done indoors, use pots or boxes. Fill these with finely sieved potting compost, which should be mixed with sharp sand and peat-moss. Seed should not be sown deeper than its own size. Ways of sowing seeds are explained with individual plants.

Taking cuttings of house plants   Most plants can be propagated from cuttings. The nurseryman does this. Some cuttings will root in a small jam jar filled with water after which they can be potted up. They can also be started in a small pot filled with sandy soil.

12

Cuttings can be placed in full light but not in the direct sun. How and when to take cuttings is given under individual plants.

Many growing agents are now used to stimulate cuttings. They can be bought at the seedsman's and the directions on the package should be observed closely. The cuttings should then root more easily and quickly.

House plants in the garden   When spring arrives, there are plenty of flowers available and pot plants usually have to take second place. Many varieties can be plunged in the garden in their pots during the second half of May. Most cacti and succulents survive readily out-of-doors but need a sunny spot. Neither they nor most other house plants need direct sunlight in the garden, since they are not used to it when indoors. Bougainvillea, Coleus and Geraniums (Pelargoniums) require full sunlight. Many other varieties thrive when they have some sun but they require a certain amount of shade during the hottest part of the day. Do not forget to water your plants regularly. A light shower is totally inadequate for a plant in full growth and you have to give it additional water. Do not forget to syringe as well specially on hot days, as it will help the plant to grow well. Feeding which was started indoors, must be carried on in the garden. Do not leave your plants outside after the beginning of October, as the nights may then become too cold and too wet. It is of great importance to lift your pots of plants every other week out of the soil and turn them, otherwise the roots will grow out of the bottom of the pot as well as growing over the sides. This can cause a great loss of leaves when the pots are lifted in October.

Dividing   If you wish to increase your plants it is possible to divide them. This can be done with the Maranta, Arums, Calathea (Zebra-plant), Anthurium (Flamingo-flower), Selaginella (Club moss), Sansevieria (Bowstring-hemp, Angola-hemp), Clivia, Bromeliads and many others.

Moisten the soil in the pot. Take the plant out of its pot and pull it apart by hand into as many parts as possible; sometimes you will have to use a knife. After this each part can be potted separately.

Layering (Aerial)   This can be done to plants which have grown too tall, particularly with plants with a woody or thick stem such as the Ficus (India-rubber plant) or the Fatsia (Japanese Aralia or 'Figleaf-palm'). An incision of not more than $\frac{1}{4}$ inch deep lengthwise is made at the desired height and the incision is kept open by a small wedge. A wad of moist peat-moss is wrapped around it and the whole covered by a plastic bag. The moss must be kept moist. As soon as roots become visible in the moss, cut off the top part of the plant and pot it in a good quality potting compost.

Miniature greenhouse   At the present time miniature greenhouses are available, both with and without heating. In these greenhouses in miniature you require trays filled with moist peat-moss. All kinds of plants can be grown in them from the middle of May onwards. It is fun to be able to sow in them, early in the season, your own seeds in pots or seedboxes. Garden flowers and annuals can also be sown in this way as well as house plants. They will come up as early as mid-May after which they may be transplanted at once into the garden. Your local dealer should be able to tell you where you can buy a miniature greenhouse. If you are interested in making your own go and look at one and no doubt you will be able to do it yourself and save a good deal of expense.

Heated miniature greenhouses are even better. You can keep house plants in them during wintertime. There are methods of heating about which the manufacturer will advise you. The kind of heating largely depends on the use you are going to make of your miniature greenhouse during the winter.

In a heated miniature greenhouse you can grow many types of plants including tropical ones, which are usually too difficult for indoor growing. Orchids, for example, do very well. Plants propagated by division need a lot of humid heat and are admirably suited to this greenhouse. Propagation from cuttings is made easier when using the miniature greenhouse.

House Plants in Bowls Nowadays we frequently see house plants grouped and planted in large bowls and they look splendid. Various shades of green foliage blend well together. The bowl must first be filled with good quality potting compost; allow a generous space at the top, otherwise when you water it splashes everywhere. Combine plants which complement each other and not, for example, cacti or succulents with foliage plants. Cacti and succulents do not need much water but foliage plants do and consequently they do not live together happily. Firm the soil in the bowl and only put in plants which have approximately the same requirement in sunlight. A nurseryman would advise you in the composition of your bowl.

Consider also the temperature and avoid a combination of plants which have different requirements. If this appears to be difficult this book should help you to select varieties with the same needs. Do not combine flowering plants with foliage varieties.

Flowering plants often look unattractive after flowering and could then spoil the appearance of the bowl.

Abutilon (Flowering maple)

1   There are many different varieties of Abutilon: the leaves are either green or mottled with gold. Nearly all bloom with colourful, bellshaped fiowers in many different shades. The plant is easy to grow and will flower practically throughout the year. During the summer it starts to bear many flowers which continue to appear well into the autumn. Keep the plant growing throughout the winter until it stops flowering, then reduce the quantity of water and cease to add liquid manure.

All Abutilon varieties grow very tall and therefore need heavy cutting back in the spring, when the plant should also be re-potted. Use a good quality potting compost, firm the plant in and do not forget to place broken crocks at the bottom of the flower-pot. Propagation can be done quite easily by using as the cuttings the new shoots which have been removed in cutting back. These should be about 4 inches long and will root if placed in a sandy soil. If a young cutting grows well it should have the top shoot nipped out to encourage the plant to become bushy and become more compact in growth. Abutilon can be placed in full sun both in summer and winter and only a little protection is needed during the hottest part of the day. It should be watered freely. The plant can be plunged in the garden in its pot during the second half of May and can remain there until mid-October when it should be taken back indoors. It should first be put in an unheated room and later in a moderate heat.

Acacia armata (Kangaroo thorn)

2   This will do well in a moderately heated room. The plant is a native of Australia where it reaches a considerable height and consequently needs cutting back as an indoor plant. It bears lovely yellow flowers in April-May. If the plant grows too high or wide it should be cut back immediately after flowering to the required size. Repot immediately after cutting back, using a good quality potting compost mixed with a little sharp sand. Do not forget the broken crocks at the bottom of the flower-pot and firm the soil well. The plant can stand a fair amount of water and it is therefore necessary to keep the soil damp. Six weeks after repotting one should start to add a little liquid manure every week. Use a well known brand of liquid manure (one teaspoon for approximately 2 pints of water will be sufficient for about 20 plants). After flowering the plant can be plunged in the garden in its pot, in a sunny place. Do not forget to water it when it is in the garden as the plant requires a lot of water during the summer. About mid-October it must be moved back indoors. It does well in the winter months in a room which is only slightly heated. The new shoots which appear after flowering can be used as cuttings if you wish more plants. Three inch shoots can be rooted indoors in a pot. Fill the pot with a mixture of peat-moss, sharp sand and potting compost. Later the young plants should be potted individually and afterwards put into larger pots.

Acalypha hispida (red-hot cat's tail, Chenille plant)

3 At one time this plant was cultivated only in greenhouses in botanical gardens but it is now becoming very popular as a house plant. The long red flower-heads are very beautiful and are a decoration for a long time. Although it is not an easy plant to grow, considerable success is possible. It requires a very moist atmosphere and has to be syringed daily with lukewarm water. When the plant is in flower only spray the leaves. Acalypha does not require much heat and can with syringing be grown in a normally heated room. The plant itself needs a lot of water and the soil in the pot should be kept moist with warm water. It cannot stand strong sunlight and therefore needs some protection from midday sun from mid-March to mid-October.

Propagation from cuttings is very easy; young shoots approximately 3 inches long, available after pruning, will root in a small pot of sandy soil. Later the young plant will have to be repotted into a larger one. Use good quality potting compost and place a broken crock in the bottom of the flower pot. No manuring should be done during the winter months but from the spring to the autumn you should give the plant a little in liquid form. Early in spring it may be cut back lightly, when repotting can also take place firm the soil normally.

Achimenes

4   Achimenes is becoming very popular as a house plant. It must however be protected from strong sunlight. There are several varieties; the blue one is very attractive but there are splendid varieties with white, pink or red flowers. The small caterpillar-shaped tubers should be ordered early in the spring and should be grown in a large flowerpot in a rich potting compost mixed with a little peat-moss, because they like an open soil. Place the pot in a normally heated room and when the young shoots appear start watering normally. When they reach a length of about 3 inches they should be protected from too strong sunlight. The soil in the pot should be kept damp and a small amount of liquid manure given weekly.

When the plant has finished flowering (which may not be until the end of the summer) let it die back. It can then be placed in a cupboard and forgotten during the winter. In the spring the tubers can be removed from the old pot and repotted in fresh compost. Sometimes Achimenes may have very weak stems, in which case it is better to give the young plants support. Some varieties are grown as hanging basket-plants.

Adiantum (Maidenhair fern)

5   Adiantum is well known as the Maidenhair fern. It is an attractive and delicate plant with finely divided foliage. Florists often use this in decorative arrangements and displays. The plant is very easy to grow. It used to be considered that the Adiantum needed a high temperature but it became apparent, especially during the winter, that it does not like a room with a high temperature and prefers a cool place. Like most ferns, it grows well in a moist atmosphere, which is the reason why it should be syringed daily with lukewarm water, especially if the plant is in a strongly heated room. The deep-dish method of cultivation may also be applied to it: take a deep dish, fill it with water, lower a saucer upside down so that the top emerges from the water. Place the pot on this little island, the plant is then just above but not standing in the water. In this way the atmosphere around the plant becomes much more humid.

Adiantum cannot stand strong sunlight and it must be protected from it. It does, however, need light and the ideal place is therefore a window-sill facing East. It needs repotting every springtime. Use a good quality potting compost, which should be mixed with a little peat-moss. Propagation by division is very simple and can be done at the time of repotting during the early spring. Large clumps can then be divided into many pieces. It requires a small amount of liquid manure weekly.

Aechmea fasciata (Bromeliad)

6   Not all Bromeliads can be grown well as house plants but this grey tubular-leaved species can be cultivated successfully. It is a very decorative plant even without its pink flower-head which makes a delightful contrast with the grey leaves. This type of Bromeliad flourishes in centrally heated rooms as it has an inbuilt resistance against a dry atmosphere. After flowering it is not necessary to throw the plant away as it will remain attractive for a long time. Moreover, you will have to wait for the formation of young growths, which develop after flowering at the base of the mother plant. When these are about 6 inches long they can be removed carefully, complete with roots, and potted separately. Do not use ordinary potting compost which will cause the plant to fail. Use a mixture of equal parts peat-moss, Osmunda fibre and well matured leaf mould, also mix in some sharp sand. Do not forget that these young growths must have broken crocks in the bottom of the flower-pot for drainage purposes.

This type of Bromeliad can stand a lot of heat but must be protected against too strong sunlight. Weekly doses of liquid manure help the plant to flourish. Lukewarm water may also be poured into the leaf-tubes during the winter months but don't forget to change it every week. The plant needs quite a lot of water, particularly during the summer months, but not so much during the winter months when no liquid manure is necessary.

Aechmea fulgens (Bromeliad)

7   Aechmea fulgens is also very popular as an indoor plant and is just as beautiful as Aechmea fasciata. Nearly all Bromeliads originate in tropical countries where many varieties can be seen growing wild on tree trunks and branches. For this reason they do not require much soil; even a small piece of cork bark can be used to hold the plant. In this case you must first tie a wad of moist peat-moss onto the bark. Peat-moss on its own is not sufficient and you should mix in a good fertiliser and osmunda fibre, when you should be successful.

Aechmea fulgens can flower very attractively, even though only one flowering stem is produced by each tube. At the time of flowering several small shoots form at the base of the mother plant. When these are about 6 inches long, they can be removed complete with their roots from the mother plant and potted separately in a light nutritious potting compost. Do not forget the broken crock in the bottom of the pot. Sometimes cuttings fail because they were removed too early from the mother plant, so leave them to develop until they are the required length.

Nearly all Bromeliads should be in a heated room. They need protection against strong sunlight, yet during the winter they enjoy a sunny place. Robust plants may be fed once a week with diluted liquid house plant manure. The soil in the pot should be kept relatively moist.

Agave americana

8 The Agaves are true succulents. Some specimens may grow to a tremendous size. They may be seen in Southern Europe growing on rocky slopes, sometimes flowering with stems of 10 to 14 feet high. Some Agave americanas have bluish leaves, others yellow variegated leaves. Even though the plants may become large, this is one of the best plants for indoor cultivation. Young plants are inexpensive and even easy to grow from seed. This should be done in a pot indoors in a warm room. As soon as the seedlings appear and can be handled, they should be transplanted. Later they must be potted individually in small pots. Use very rich potting compost mixed with some heavy loam. Do not forget the broken crock in the bottom of the flower-pot. Older plants form young plants at the base very readily. When these are of approximately 3 to 4 inches high, they may be removed from the mother plant, complete with roots, after which they can be potted and grown on individually.

As this is a true succulent, it does not require much water. It is sufficient to water it once every fortnight during the winter months, but it does require considerably more water during the summer. It is advisable to grow the plants in the full sun. Agave victoriae -reginae is one of the most beautiful varieties for sowing.

Aglaonema

9   This graceful foliage plant comes from Indonesia and Malaya and is similar to the better known Dieffenbachia (Dumb Cane). There are some varieties which are cultivated as house plants and these require a humid atmosphere, although normal room temperature is adequate. Frequent syringing is necessary, specially during the winter months, and lukewarm water is essential. The soil in the pot should be kept damp.

This plant cannot stand the bright sunshine of the summer months and should therefore be partially protected from mid-April to mid-September. It does, however, need a light place. Different varieties have attractive variegated leaves which also differ in shape. The flower is insignificant but it bears afterwards beautiful red berries which last a long time. During the summer months and in early spring a light weekly feeding is necessary. Propagation by means of dividing is possible with this plant. This can best be performed during early spring. Cuttings can also be taken, but this is better done in a greenhouse than at room temperatures. Repotting should be done during early spring. Use a well known potting compost with a little additional peat-moss. The soil should be rich and well aerated. In a large plant bowl this plant can be grown successfully in combination with other tropical plants which require much heat and little sun. Aphids often appear underneath the leaves; to prevent this the leaves should be lightly sponged once a week.

Allamanda cathartica

10   This is a tropical climber with extremely lovely yellow flowers and large calyxes. The large flowers are poisonous so you must be careful to keep the plant away from small children. There are varieties with more compact growth, which are really more suitable as indoor plants but their propagation from cuttings is extremely difficult. If the plant is growing under good conditions, it will develop enormous shoots, which you must train with the aid of small sticks placed firmly in the soil. The plant will stand a fair amount of sun: it does not need protection on a window sill facing East, but grown facing South some protection must be provided during the hottest part of the day. It requires a humid atmosphere and especially before the flowers appear syringe the large leaves daily with lukewarm water. The soil in the pot should be kept moist.

As we said previously propagation by means of cuttings is not easy; the nurseryman may be successful or you may try yourself. Young shoots approximately 4 inches long should be placed in a small pot of sandy soil and covered with a plastic bag. When the cuttings have rooted, each cutting should be potted up separately. Use normal potting compost, mixed with a heavy loam. The plant should be grown in a warm room where it will flower profusely during the summer. After flowering allow the plant to rest during the winter and cut any excessively long shoots back. It needs adequate feeding, so give it liquid manure regularly, except during winter.

Aloe arborescens (Tree Aloe)

11   Succulents and cacti are very popular indoor plants. There are several attractive varieties amongst the Aloe family. The Aloe arborescens is easy to cultivate and will grow to a good size, although it will take years before it could be called a tree. Propagation is easily done from cuttings either from the pruned branches or from young shoots produced by the mother plant. The latter may be removed when they are about 6 inches long. Cuttings should be allowed to dry out for a day in a shady place so that the wound can heal. They can then be potted in small pots of sandy soil and roots will form very quickly. Usually this plant is cultivated in a small pot which means that it needs repotting to a larger size quite soon after you receive it. Fill the new pot with well known potting compost or with special cactus soil. Firm the soil well. A piece of crock should be placed in the bottom of the flower-pot, because the small hole should never be blocked.

Older specimens of this Aloe may flower very well, but remove the dead flower after flowering. The plant does not require much heat, so a very slightly heated room is sufficient. Even though it can stand the sun very well, it needs some protection from strong sunlight during the summer or black spots will develop on the leaves. Little water is required during the winter and watering once a week is then sufficient.

Aloe variegata (Partridge-breasted Aloe)

12   Wherever succulents are grown, you are sure to find the Partridge-breasted Aloe. It is a beautiful indoor plant which will give you great joy. The exquisitely marked leaves fit across each other like roof tiles. This succulent may flower during the winter and, as such, it is an exception to most other varieties. In the winter nearly all cacti and succulents pass through a resting period during which a flowering stem is formed. Since they are not growing actively, they do not have to be watered regularly. It is sufficient to keep the soil moist.

Aloe can be grown from seed, which should be sown indoors early in spring or during the summer months. Fill the pot with finely sieved potting compost, scatter the seeds and cover them over lightly. Place a sheet of glass and a sheet of paper on top to prevent drying out of the soil. Remove both when the young seedlings appear as they require full light at once. Later they should be pricked out and when they are well established they can be transferred to small pots. Propagation from new shoots is not difficult either. When the plant becomes a little older they form at the base of the mother plant and can be easily removed, complete with roots. Protect the plant during the summer against the full sun. If repotting has to take place, do this in the early summer but in any case immediately after flowering.

Ampelopsis brevipedunculata elegans

13 It is difficult to remember the Latin name of this plant, but every florist stocks it. The red-grey leaves are very attractive and it makes a handsome hanging plant. It does not require much heat and can grow in an unheated but frost-free room, although it does do better in a warm room. The best time to buy this plant is in the spring when the new leaves come out and the plant looks particularly attractive. The plant can stand full sunlight but it does need a lot of watering and should be syringed regularly. It can be propagated readily from cuttings of young shoots. These should be about 3 inches long and when placed in a jam jar of water roots will form and the cuttings can be potted up later on. When they are well established they need to be potted on in larger pots.

From mid-May until mid-October the plant can be plunged in the garden in its pot. Choose a sunny spot and do not forget to water it. When the plant is taken back indoors growing may continue until mid-December when no more manure should be given. During the winter give very little water as the plant should rest for a few weeks and it will lose all its leaves. Early in the spring the bare stems can be pruned drastically and the plant can be repotted. Use good quality potting soil and do not forget the crock in the bottom of the pot. Ampelopsis henryana can also be grown as an indoor plant but this variety needs more warmth.

Ananas comosus (Pineapple)

14   The pineapple is grown in the tropics as a commercial plant and its large fruits are well known. People who have lived in the tropics will know the plant and will realize the amount of sun it requires. However, it is possible to cultivate the plant over here and in hothouses it may produce good and tasty fruits. There is also a variety with yellowish-red leaves which may be grown as a decorative house plant. You may succeed in producing a fruit, but do not expect too much!

This coloured pineapple variety may be a little difficult to buy, but they are becoming more readily available. Choose a sturdy plant and allow it plenty of room, because it needs it. As the leaves are sharply toothed, take care that the curtains do not get caught in them. The plant grows well in a sunny garden room, but it must be kept in a warm one. It can stand the sun during the summer time but a little protection is needed during the hottest part of the day. When the plant gets older a flower stem will form and eventually a small fruit. This is the end of the old plant but sufficient young side shoots should have formed by then at the base of the mother plant for propagation. They can be removed complete with roots from the mother plant. The pineapple needs heavy soil, and the potting compost to be used should also be mixed with some heavy loam.

Anthurium andreanum (Lakanthurium)

15 The exquisite flowers of the Lakanthurium can be seen in most florists' shops. It is strange that they are so popular as cut flowers, yet lesser known as house plants. They appear in all possible colours, there are even varieties with green flowers. Some varieties have enormous flowers. The reason why this plant is not grown so much may be due to its size. It requires a good deal of space and should really be grown in a spacious bay-window.

The plant requires, as all Flamingo flowers, a very moist atmosphere and they need an even higher temperature than Anthurium scherzerianum. When the plant matures, it will form aerial roots which should not be removed. If they become a nuisance bury them in the soil of the pot. Lakanthurium requires a large pot which should be one third full of broken crocks. The soil mixture should be well aerated and consist of a mixture of de-composed leaf mould, peat-moss and osmunda fibre with the addition of some rotted cow manure if available. Wait until flowering has finished before repotting. Protect the plant against strong sunlight during the summer, but in winter the plant will thrive in a sunny place. Propagation by division is possible, particularly when the plant is not in flower. Young shoots are formed at the base of the plant and these may be removed complete with roots and grown on in separate pots.

Anthurium crystallinum

16   This is really a hothouse plant even though it is also grown successfully as a house plant. The leaves are bronze-green in colour when young, later becoming bright green with a velvety sheen and with pale grey veins. This plant is very popular in Denmark and Sweden as an indoor plant. The flower bract is green and it is better to remove the flower-head as the plant will then grow much better. It is a plant which needs a good deal of warmth and plenty of moisture and therefore is excellently suited for growing in a centrally heated room. The beautiful leaf must be syringed daily with lukewarm water. The soil in the pot should be kept fairly moist. The plant should benefit from the deep-dish method which would make the air around it much more humid. Propagation is not very easy. The nurseryman uses seed, but this will not be very successful indoors. Division is possible with large, well-established plants. They can be removed from the pot early in spring and divided into sections, each section having a leaf or a young shoot. The soil mixture should be nutritious and well aerated. Mix some peat-moss and leaf-mould with the potting compost. The plant cannot stand much sun, it therefore needs protection during the summer months even in East-facing windows, but during wintertime it thrives in a sunny place. The plant appreciates plenty of feeding and should be given liquid manure during spring and summer once a week.

Anthurium scherzerianum (Flamingo flower)

17   A very profuse flowering evergreen house plant. It requires a normally heated room and a very humid atmosphere. You will obtain the best results with the so-called deep-dish method. Take a deep dish and place a saucer upside down in it. Fill the dish with water up to the top of the saucer. The pot is placed on the saucer and it is now just above the water but not actually in it. The atmosphere around the plant is thereby much more humid, but it is still necessary to syringe the leaves daily with lukewarm water.

The potting compost should be kept moist and it is useful to cover it with a small layer of peat-moss, which you can buy at a florist's. The Flamingo flower may flower for most of the year but when no new flowerbuds appear it will need a rest and feeding should stop. It is better to pot on immediately after flowering and not when you are expecting new flowerbuds. Do not use a good potting compost for this, as it would be too rich. The compost should be a mixture of mature leaf soil, some rough peat and fibrous loam. You may be able to buy the mixture ready-made at a nurseryman's. Propagation by division can be done at the same time as the repotting. The plant needs protection against strong sunlight. There are deep-red and orange-red varieties both of which are extremely beautiful. You will be able to enjoy these attractive flowers for a long time.

Aphelandra squarrosa Leopoldii

18   The name of this plant is less well-known than the plant itself. Aphelandra Leopoldii is one of the most popular varieties. It has yellow flowers, but there are others with orange flowers. They all need a very moist atmosphere and protection from strong sunlight. Cultivation is most successful in a normally heated room because they like humidity and warmth. It is perhaps best to grow them by the so-called deep-dish method: take a deep dish, fill it with water, insert a saucer upside down so that the bottom part just penetrates the water surface. Place the pot on this and it will now be just above the water level, but not actually in it. This makes the atmosphere around the plant much more humid but it still needs a daily syringe with lukewarm water.

Aphelandra is not an easy plant; after flowering it often sheds some of its beautiful leaves. This may be prevented by using lukewarm water for watering. Never use cold tapwater for this plant but add some hot water to make it tepid. After flowering, cut the flower stem away and give it a rest of approximately 6 weeks, do not feed it and give only sufficient water to retain the foliage. In early spring you should cut it back as required and repot it in a potting compost. When the plant has become established give it its weekly small ration of liquid manure. Propagation from cuttings is possible but it is rather difficult to do in the house.

Araucaria heterophylla (Norfolk Island Pine)

19 This is a tender evergreen coniferous tree, which, although not so popular now, was traditionally given as a wedding present in Holland. If treated well, it can live for years. This plant was introduced during the late eighteenth century and you should be able to acquire it at a good florist's.

A normally heated room is too warm for this plant; the beautiful green tiers will drop one by one if it is kept too warm and the decorative effect will be lost. It thrives in a moderately heated room; during the winter the plant appreciates a sunny position but it must be placed so that the leaves are not touched as needles are very delicate. The fibrous root system dries out much sooner than would be expected and the soil in the pot should therefore be kept moist. It is best to give a little diluted liquid manure once every fortnight. Dissolve one teaspoon in two pints of water - a sufficient quantity for approximately 20 indoor plants. During the summer months it can be plunged in the garden, in its pot. It requires a sheltered spot, shaded during the hottest part of the day. In some parts of the world this attractive house plant grows to enormous height; specimens in the Canary islands have grown to over 80 feet high.

Ardisia crispa

20 An attractive evergreen plant, a native of the East Indies and first introduced during the early nineteenth century. Its flowering period during the summer is not its most pleasant stage, but afterwards numerous pea-sized berries develop, which are bright red and can be decorative all through the winter and well into the spring. To achieve this, you must not keep it too warm as the plant cannot stand dry heat. Regular syringing is advisable, but not while it is flowering. Use tepid water for syringing. It is best kept in a moderately heated room, even normal room temperature is rather too much for it. The soil in the pot should be kept moist and a small addition of manure every other week is beneficial. Use a well-known liquid manure recommended for house plants.

When necessary plants which have grown too large can be cut back. Do this when the berries have dried up and do not be too severe. Potting on can take place at the same time. Use normal potting compost, firm well and do not forget the crock in the bottom of the pot. This plant loves sunshine and only needs a little protection during the hottest part of the day. Florists propagate this plant from seed and cuttings. Seed is the best method, which you should do in a miniature heated greenhouse. Sometimes the seedlings become rather straggly and should be staked, cuttings usually remaining rather bushier.

Aregelia (Neoregelia-Bromelia)

21 Only a few members of the Aregelia family are cultivated. They belong to the Bromeliad group, which are easily recognized from their characteristic appearance and type of flower. Aregelia carolinae is one of the best varieties and is most pleasing as an indoor plant. The leaves are dark green and the edges are bordered with spines. While the plant is in flower the upper leaves turn into a beautiful dull purple although the small white, tubular flowers are insignificant. There is another variety with a multi-coloured leaf. As with most Bromeliads, flowering takes place only once from the same growth which in this case is a rosette. However, after flowering the plant remains attractive for some years. Further flowers depend on the young shoots which form at the base of the mother plant. When these are 3 to 4 inches high, they should be removed carefully with their roots and be grown on individually. Once the young plants are doing well, the mother plant can be thrown away. The plant requires a normally heated room and protection against too fierce sunlight is necessary. A nutritious but well aerated soil mixture is necessary, so make a compost with peat-moss and Osmunda fibre. Do not forget the crocks at the bottom of the pot. You will enjoy this plant, especially in a light room. Keep the soil in the pot moist and water with tepid water. When not in flower, it is useful to dribble a little water occasionally into the centre of the leaves.

Asparagus plumosus (Asparagus Fern)

22   This is a popular indoor plant, well-known as the Asparagus Fern. People usually consider that it is a small plant and nurserymen may supply it in too small a pot which means that repotting will soon be necessary. Use a normal potting compost but add a little peatmoss and well rotted cow manure as the plant prefers nutritious but well aerated soil. Often the florist uses this plant in decorative arrangements or in a bowl together with other plants. The Asparagus will usually outlive the other plants and can be taken out and grown separately. It is well suited to normal living room temperatures but flourishes in a slightly warmer temperature. Continental florists use this plant solely for its decorative green foliage and large nurseries concentrate on the cultivation of this one plant. It is frequently used for table decorations and button-holes.

The plant needs protection against the sun but requires a light place. Keep the soil in the pot moist; the larger plants should have a weekly dose of liquid manure. If necessary, repotting can take place in the early spring. Use a normal potting compost. Propagate by division, which can be done at the same time as the repotting in the early spring. Syringing is most benificial and should be done, particularly during the winter, in a heated room.

Asparagus sprengeri (Asparagus)

23   This is a very well known, evergreen house plant, used extensively by florists for use in decorative arrangements. In Europe there are growers who concentrate on the cultivation of such varieties, as the long tendrils are extremely useful for table decorations and in bouquets. As a house plant, this variety is easy to grow. Keep it in a cool place; normal room temperatures are really a little too much for the plant which prefers only a slightly heated room. If the Asparagus is given to you in a small pot, you will probably soon need to repot it. Use normal potting compost but do not forget to add a little manure, as the plant needs a lot of nourishment. Older plants, especially those which have not been repotted, must have their weekly ration of liquid manure. Use a well-known liquid house plant manure. One teaspoon for two pints of water is sufficient for approximately 20 plants. Asparagus needs plenty of water and the soil in the pot has to be kept very moist. During the winter the plant goes through a period of rest when manuring should be stopped and watering should be reduced. Repotting may take place during the early spring. Propagation is by division, which can be done at the same time as the repotting. Seed sowing can also be successful in a small pot in a warm room. At a later stage the small plants can be grown on separately. The seeds have to be filed lightly before sowing, as they are very hard.

Aspidistra lurida (elatior)

24 I do not think that there exists an easier plant to grow than the Aspidistra, as it requires almost no attention. The main reason for growing it is the attractive foliage. There is also a variegated variety, with alternate longitudinal stripes to the leaves but the plain coloured variety is stronger and it can be placed in a dark corner or in a rather cold hall, where it will flourish equally well. It is popular for use in displays of indoor plants, where it forms an effective background, even in contemporary surroundings. Although it is not often realised, the Aspidistra does flower, with brown-grey, rosette-shaped flowers produced near the ground and lying almost flat on it. The plant needs little attention apart from normal watering. Syringing is beneficial but it is even better to wipe the large tall leaves every other week with a moist sponge. Nourishment is appreciated and a little manuring every fortnight is beneficial. Use a well-known house plant manure. The plant can stand the sun but it generally prefers shade. Propagation is by division of the roots only and this should be done preferably in the early spring. Moisten the soil in the pot and remove the plant, carefully divide the root stock, each section complete with some roots and leaves should be put in a small pot. The plain green variety cannot stand as much sunlight as the variegated one. When the plant becomes very large it can still be very decorative when planted in a wooden tub.

Asplenium nidus (Bird's-nest Fern)

25 This is a very decorative fern and the plant will remain so for many years. It should be grown in a normally heated room. Many ferns originate in tropical forests. In its native surroundings, this plant grows high up in the trees, and therefore requires humidity and warmth. It is usual to moisten the leaves daily by syringing them with tepid water: never use cold tapwater. The rather large leaves may grow very wide and consequently require plenty of space. During the summer, water freely and occasionally pour some tepid water down the centre of the plant. It should be kept growing during the winter. During the summer a weekly ration of a little diluted house-plant manure is required; during the winter give this every alternate week. If repotting is required, wait until the early spring, which is the ideal time. Use a good quality potting compost and add a little peat-moss. Place a crock in the bottom of the pot so that the hole does not get blocked up with soil. This fern is often troubled by the arrival of small brown wood lice. You may know one remedy which is to touch them lightly with undiluted methylated spirit. There are also efficient sprays available. The plant needs protection against the sun from mid-March to mid-September. If the situation of the fern is too cold or too damp, brown spots will appear on the new leaves and also the edges will become affected. If the atmosphere is too dry, the edges of the leaves will tear.

Astrophytum myriostigma (Bishop's mitre)

26   In the Astrophytum group there are four major varieties of which the Bishop's mitre is the best known. The Bishop's mitre is decorated with numerous minute white dots and gets its name from the five definite ridges which form the plant. Do not forget the Astrophytum needs a porous soil rich in lime and a layer of gravel or chips of stone in the bottom of the pot. The Bishop's mitre can stand a lot of sun but needs a little protection during the hottest part of the day. During the winter it should be in a sunny position. This cactus flowers well, the plain yellow flowers developing from the centre of the plant. During the winter the plant should not be in too warm a position, a moderately heated room is sufficient for it. In this cool environment the water requirement is greatly reduced: moisten the soil with a little water every two weeks only. Do not spray. During the summer it is sufficient to water it more freely on alternate days.

If repotting is necessary, the best time to do it is in the early spring. Astrophytums are completely different from other types of cactus and will attract immediate attention in a collection. It can be propagated from seed in a pot indoors in a sandy soil mixture. After germination the seedling soon needs to be repotted, preferably in a sandy soil mixture, and eventually every seedling will require its own individual small pot.

Aucuba japonica variegata (Spotted Laurel or Variegated Laurel)

27   The Aucuba is an evergreen shrub really more suitable for the garden than indoors, where it is better considered a temporary visitor. Besides the variegated species, there is the plain green variety, of the two the former is more attractive for indoor cultivation. Excellent plants can be grown in normally heated rooms. To achieve this, sponge the leaves weekly with a moist sponge and spray daily with tepid water. Keep the soil in the pot well watered. This plant does extremely well in unheated but frost free rooms. The green variety is even easier to grow and can effectively be kept in a cool, dark hall, even though it appreciates a lighter position.

If the atmosphere is too dry, the plant starts to shed its leaves. This will happen to some degree in any case during the winter. During early spring the plant can be trimmed and repotted, using ordinary good quality potting compost. Propagation can be done by taking cuttings; use a sandy compost which is particularly suitable for the rooting of cuttings and is freely available in shops.

If the plant is reluctant to grow, it should be planted out of doors but in a very shady position and never in the autumn or winter. It needs plenty of space because it will develop to a sizeable shrub.

Begonia corallina

28 The name Begonia was given to the whole family in honour of Michel Begon, who was a patron of Botany and a Governor of Canada. The Begonia corallina is a popular indoor variety. It needs plenty of space as it grows quite wide and tall.

This variety is one of the most beautiful of the Begonia family. The large leaves are grey-flecked, and it has large bunches of pinkish flowers. It flowers very easily, practically throughout the year, except for the depth of winter. The plant sometimes gives reason for anxiety when large leaves drop for no apparent reason. The only remedy seems to be to spray lightly every day with tepid water. As the plant may grow very high, it is essential to give it nourishment. A weekly addition of liquid manure is sufficient, but this is not necessary during the winter. The leaves tend to drop, especially when the winter is approaching, and you must then give the plant a light or sunny position. However, during the summer it needs protection against the sun. If many leaves are shed in the winter, the plant should be cut back vigorously, especially if the stems are bare of leaves. Young shoots may be used as cuttings. When they are approximately 6 inches long, remove them and place them in a jam jar filled with water, where they will root. When there are sufficient roots, each cutting can be potted separately. Use a well-known potting compost. The plant is very decorative and needs a slightly heated room during the winter.

Begonia Gloire de Lorraine (Winter flowering Begonia)

29 The many varieties of winter-flowering Begonias are favourite decorative plants for winter displays indoors or in conservatories. Eges Favorite with its numerous pale pink flowers is extremely attractive. This is practically the only variety which does not drop its flowers quickly. The varieties with the large flowers are exquisite but sometimes drop all open flowers and buds after a few days. This can be prevented by leaving the plant undisturbed. Leave it in a normally heated room (a slightly warm room is also adequate), do not turn the pot (it is better to mark the front of the pot so that it can be replaced in exactly the same position). Leaf and bud shedding is also aggravated by watering with cold tap water. Although tap water itself is not harmful, the cold water on the roots causes the damage. Always mix it with sufficient hot water to make it tepid. Adding water to the saucer on which the plant stands is all right, so is watering on top of the soil. However, if there is still water left on the saucer a quarter of an hour after watering, it should be removed. Do not leave any water in the bottom of a decorative overpot. If the plant is first potted in high quality potting compost and you wish it to flower constantly, it is necessary to give it some additional nourishment. It can be applied as a weekly dose of diluted liquid manure. The plant needs a light position but must be shielded against the sun from the early spring onwards. It is possible to keep the Begonia until the next season but the plant must be cut back drastically after flowering and then repotted into good potting compost.

Begonia metallica

30   The name is so appropriate for this Begonia variety, it is a really bushy plant with metallic, bronze-green foliage. It may grow to considerable height and therefore needs plenty of space. The flowers, although pretty, are pale pink and not as striking as in some Begonias. Propagation is simply done by taking cuttings. This can be done during the early spring when the mature plant needs cutting back. Cuttings of about 4 inches are ideal. Put them in a small pot with soil consisting of sand and peat-mould in which they will root very quickly. Each cutting will have to be reared separately, and a change of soil is required, for which the normal potting compost should be used. During the summer the plant will have to be repotted several times.

The plant needs a shady position and even if placed on a window sill facing East protection is needed during the summer. Water freely and spray regularly with tepid water. The plant flourishes in a moderately heated room. Early spring is the best time for cutting the plant back vigorously and simultaneously repotting it, using good quality potting compost. Six weeks after repotting, you should start to give it a small dose of liquid manure, using diluted house plant manure. If you like a nice bushy plant, then the tops must be cut out several times when the young plant is well established.

Begonia rex

31   This Begonia is the principal source of a magnificent range of indoor Begonias. The leaves are wrinkled, dark olive green with a metallic sheen and a broad silver white zone parallel to and about 1 inch inside the margin. They are easy-going indoor plants, which you can cultivate without any trouble.

They grow best at temperatures between 60 and 68° and in a very moist atmosphere. The deep-dish method helps to provide these conditions: take a deep dish and place a saucer upside down in it, then add water so that the bottom of the saucer just emerges from the water surface. Place the pot on this, the plant is now just above the water but not in it and thrives in the increased humidity. This is extremely important as the plant should not be sprayed as this encourages the formation of brown patches on the leaves. Begonias are usually supplied in very small pots and should be repotted soon after buying. Mix the potting compost with a little additional leaf-mould as this plant needs a nutritious but well aerated soil. Do not forget to put crocks in the bottom of the pot. Although most Begonias flower, the main attraction of this one is its beautiful leaves. It can be increased by leaf propagation. The leaves are cut with a sharp knife into approximately 1 inch squares. These are placed on a shallow pan with white sand and then covered with glass and a sheet of paper. Place the pan in a very warm position and keep the sand moist. When the roots have formed, the small plants will develop and the glass and paper can be removed.

Begonia semperflorens (Summer flowering Begonia)

32 Begonia semperflorens is a very adaptable plant. It can flower throughout the year and can be cultivated both indoors and in the garden. There are several varieties which have either red, pink or white flowers. The red variety is very attractive and usually has dark brown leaves.

Begonia semperflorens can be grown in a normally or slightly heated room, it likes plenty of sun but a little protection is required during the hottest part of the day, although this is not necessary in a window facing East.

The plant requires to be watered freely; the soil in the pot should be kept moist. However, it is better not to spray. During the winter it may lose some leaves, but this can be prevented by placing the plant on a window-sill facing South. Should this be unsuccessful, then you may cut the plant back a little during the spring and repot it. Use a normal potting compost enriched with some peat-mould as the plant likes nutritious but well aerated soil. Propagation is achieved by taking cuttings; young shoots of approximately 3 inches will root easily in a jam jar of water and they can be potted later. During the summer the plant will do well in the garden. Towards October it must be taken indoors into a slightly heated room and potted in a good compost. The florist may propagate it from seeds, but this is done during the spring.

Begonia tuberous-rooted hybrids

33 These Begonias are suitable both for the garden and for indoor growing. They are extremely decorative plants and thrive well in indoor plant boxes. There are many varieties with large and small flowers, double and single flowers and in many different colours.

Plants can be bought fullgrown, in flower. If you prefer to grow them yourself, you may buy the tubers in January, when they should be placed dry in a box with aerated soil. Place the tubers just under the surface. Take the box in a heated room, cover it over with a sheet of glass and keep the soil moist. When young shoots appear, the glass may be removed. When the shoots are growing, the heat must be reduced and when they reach a length of approximately 4 inches, each tuber must be potted in an ordinary sized flower pot. Use a normal potting compost with a little additional peat-mould. Keep in full sun until mid-April. When the sun becomes stronger, protection is needed, but this is not necessary on a window sill facing East. The plant requires plenty of water, but do not spray it when it is in full flower. Let the plant die down after flowering, leave the tuber in the pot and put it away dry. Take the tuber up in early spring and pot again.

Beloperone guttata (Shrimp Plant)

34 The Shrimp Plant can be recognized at once by its special flowering head which is composed of overlapping ear-shaped bracts. The flowers themselves are insignificant, they soon die and only a few flowers open simultaneously. The pale red bracts are the main decorative contribution of the plant.

You will enjoy the Beloperone because during the greater part of the summer it bears these attractive bracts. The plant does not flower during the winter and therefore does not require much heat. It can be left in a slightly heated room, even if the room is only just frost free. It should not be manured and watering can be reduced during the winter. The plant will lose many of its leaves but that is no reason to worry. In early spring the bare branches can be cut back and the plant can be repotted at the same time. Use good quality potting compost, do not forget to put a crock in the bottom of the pot because the drainage hole must not be blocked. When repotted, the plant may be placed in a warmer position and watered more freely. It does well in a situation with some sun, particularly on a window sill facing East. Propagation is easily achieved from taking cuttings, which is best done during the spring. When the plant has been cut back, young shoots can be placed in a jam jar filled with water for rooting purposes.

Bougainvillea glabra var. sanderiana

35 This plant is a native of South America and was named after the French navigator Bougainville. It is very popular in the South of Europe where it is an attractive climber on the white walls of the houses. The beautiful violet-mauve bracts are very striking but nowadays there are even varieties with salmon and red bracts. The flowers are small and vary from white to pale yellow.

It really is a difficult plant to grow and it drops its leaves and flowers on the slightest provocation. The Bougainvillea prefers a window facing East but when in full flower a little protection from sunlight is necessary. Florists may be successful and produce flowers at any time of the year, but the normal time is in the early summer. After flowering the plant can be removed to the garden complete with pot, and plunged in a very warm and sunny spot. Do not forget to water it and trim the plant back after flowering. As it is a climber, it may suddenly develop very long shoots, which must be pruned when repotting. Use a well known potting compost enriched with some rotted cow manure and heavy loam, as this plant requires a firm soil mixture.

Towards the end of September the plant should be brought back indoors, at first to an unheated room. After a while a little warmth is required. Water infrequently, allowing the leaves to drop and in February encourage growth by liberal spraying and watering. You can then give a weekly dose of a little diluted liquid manure and your plant will flower profusely annually in early summer.

Browallia

36 A plant which flowers readily, the family being first introduced in the mid-eighteenth century from moderately warm regions. It can be raised from seed though it may be a little hard to find the seed (though you may see it offered in any good seed catalogue). Sow the seeds immediately after receiving them in a pot indoors. Use finely sieved sandy potting compost and sow 1/16 inch deep, just below the surface, in March. Cover the pot with a sheet of glass and paper. Keep the pot in a warm room and keep the soil moist by spraying with water. When the seedlings appear, remove the glass and paper and, when this is possible, transplant three or four into a 5 inch pot with good potting compost. When they are well established repot them in a larger pot in good potting compost. It is necessary to pinch out the tops of the stems a few times to obtain a well shaped plant. The plant needs a sunny position, but a little protection during the hottest part of the day. Water freely and apply diluted liquid manure once a week. The blue flowers are very attractive and it is possible to keep the plant flowering in summer and winter time. Non-flowering plants should be kept in a moderately warm room and sprayed with tepid water. It can be propagated by taking young shoots which were pinched out using them as cuttings. They readily form roots.

Brunfelsia (Franciscea)

37 The Brunfelsia is a warm greenhouse evergreen flowering shrub, with exquisite flowers which decorate the plant for a fairly long time. This is why it is such a challenge to keep this plant until it flowers, but it is difficult and requires great care and attention. The main mistake made during cultivation is that the plant is generally kept too warm. It is much happier in a cool room than in a normally heated room.

Flowering can occur at any time of the year, but most frequently in early spring and early summer. Although the plant likes sunshine, after the beginning of April protection against bright sunlight is essential. This is not necessary if it is grown on a window-sill facing East. After flowering the plant needs a resting period. Do not apply manure for about six weeks, then only a small amount of diluted liquid manure should be applied. If necessary, the plant may be plunged in the garden in its pot for the summer. Find a sheltered spot, where there is some shade during the hottest part of the day. It can be propagated by taking cuttings but use a recommended potting compost. Slight pruning after flowering is beneficial but do not overdo it because the plant does not readily form new shoots.

Caladium

38   This decorative tropical plant is very popular nowadays. The leaves are arrow-shaped and marked in many colours and patterns. Some varieties have white leaves, but there are others with a rich variety of coloured foliage. This is a plant which requires a warm humid atmosphere and is very successfully grown with the deep-dish method. Put some water in a deep dish, place a saucer upside down in the centre so that the top just emerges and place the pot on it. The plant is now just above the water surface but not in it. Caladiums belong to a very delicate group of house plants known as stove or hothouse plants, they are members of the Arum family, which can be seen from the leaves. The first leaves to appear are green and the same in shape, but as they are not very attractive it is better to remove them as they appear.

The Caladium needs plenty of sun and only a little shading during the hottest part of the day. Regular spraying is necessary using tepid water. The soil in the pot must be kept moist. The plant needs plenty of nourishment. A small addition every week is useful, using liquid house plant manure.

Once the leaves have died down, put the plant in a cupboard and forget it during the winter. When early spring arrives, the tubers must be removed from the soil and repotted in fresh potting compost. Place the plant in a heated room and keep the soil moist: very soon the decorative leaves will develop once more. You will enjoy the Caladium for years.

Calathea makoyana (Maranta) (Peacock plant)

39   The beauty of the leaves, which are patterned on both sides, immediately indicates that this is close to Maranta. It is slow in growth and requires a very warm humid atmosphere. The colourful foliage should be sprayed daily with tepid water. Keep the soil in the pot moist. The plant will shed some leaves, especially during the wintertime. As the atmosphere will be too dry when this happens, increase the spraying. The best way to cultivate this plant is the deep-dish method: fill a deep dish with enough water to cover an upside down saucer until only the top emerges from the water. Place the pot on this little island, the plant is now just above the water but not in it and it will profit by the humid atmosphere around it. Calathea needs special protection against the sun, mainly from mid-March to mid-October but it requires a light place. The plant needs a good deal of nourishment and should be manured once a week. Use the normal liquid house plant manure.

The plant can be propagated by dividing it early in the spring. Old plants are removed from the pot and carefully divided, each section is then cultivated individually. Use a well-known potting compost but add a good amount of peat-mould, as the plant likes a light well-aerated soil. Place some crocks at the bottom of the pot. The best results are achieved with shallow pots. If you have only deep pots, fill the bottom half with broken crocks.

Calceolaria (Slipper-flower, Slipper-wort)

40   You will enjoy your Slipper-plant, as it is a very pleasing flowering plant which is available in many colours. It is very tempting to buy the plant in full flower but it is much better to take one with only a very few flowers open and many buds which will keep much longer. The florist will have them in full flower early in the spring. Remember that this plant has been brought along with very little heat and the living room will be far too hot. A very moderately heated room or a frost-free place is all that is required. From April onwards protection is needed from the sun, otherwise the leaves will wilt or burn.

Keep the soil in the pot moist and spray the plant except when it is in flower. A weekly dose of a little diluted liquid manure is necessary until the plant is in full flower. It is very succeptible to draught, try to avoid this, otherwise it will be covered at once with aphids. This also occurs when the plant is cultivated in a place which is too hot. If aphids do occur, use an anti-aphid spray. Repeat this after 10 days. It is possible to keep the Slipper -plant till the next season but it needs a great deal of trouble and care and the result achieved is often not satisfactory. It is much better to order a new plant in early spring. The florist grows them from seed, which he sows in July-August.

Callisia elegans

41   This is a very elegant, decorative plant which is generally thought to belong to the Tradescantia family. It is an easy plant to keep and will give you a lot of pleasure. The plant needs plenty of sun but during the summer it needs some protection during the hottest part of the day. However, it always should have plenty of light and if it is left in a dark place during the winter the beautifully marked leaves will become too green and the decorative effect is spoilt. One attractive feature is the ease with which it is propagated from cuttings. Young shoots of about 3 inches root easily after placing them in a pot with potting compost, about five to one pot. They soon grow into a delightful plant. Propagation by division is also possible but hardly necessary as the taking of cuttings is much easier. Often the older plants will become rather bare of leaves during the winter which is one of the main reasons for making cuttings regularly.

This plant does not require much heat, so it does well in a moderately heated room. It should be freely watered, but it is better not to spray. A little liquid manure may be given weekly from early spring until late autumn. If you do not know what to do with it during the summer, just plunge the plant complete with pot in the garden and bring it back indoors towards the end of September. Little displays in bowls and trays are most attractive.

Campanula isophylla alba

42   This species of Bellflower is a very well-known house plant which flourishes under nearly all conditions. It can be cultivated on a window-sill facing East but does equally well on one facing North. When the plant is in full flower it needs a little protection against very strong sunlight. It is, of course, very tempting to buy a plant in full flower but it is much better to choose one with only a few flowers out and many buds. July or August is a suitable time to buy a plant in flower but nowadays the florists can bring them along either much earlier, or later. The florist will have supplied the plant with a good potting compost, but in order to keep it flowering and encourage new bud formation, it requires a weekly addition of liquid manure. During flowering, carefully remove all dead flowers, otherwise they will run to seed and unnecessarily weaken the plant. After flowering the stems can be pruned right back, preferably right to the top of the pot, and the plant can be kept until the next growing season in a frost-free but not too warm room. Moderate watering is needed in this cool environment and manuring must cease. Repot early in the spring, using good potting compost. Propagate by means of cuttings in the early spring. Young shoots can be cut off and put in a jam jar filled with water to root. This Bellflower can be trained as a hanging plant. There is also a variety with blue flowers.

Canna lucifer (Indian flowering reed)

43 The canna is a popular garden plant, especially in the South of France and Italy, where it can reach a height of over 5 feet. It may be grown out of doors here as well, but a beautiful summer is essential for success, and a very sunny spot must be chosen.
A miniature variety of the Canna family is Canna lucifer. It has beautiful red flowers with a yellow edge, which makes it all the more attractive. Nowadays you should be able to get it from a florist throughout the year. It is very suitable for indoor cultivation and it is one of the few house plants which enjoy full sunshine. A place on a window-sill facing South is ideal, the plant will flower there for a long period. When it goes out of flower, leave the stem for a little while, as often another bud will develop. The leaves are rather large and the plant therefore requires plenty of watering; keep the soil moist and use tepid water. When it stops flowering, you may remove the plant from the pot during the summer, and allow it to continue to grow in the garden. In the middle of October the Canna must be dug up carefully with plenty of soil, stored in a box, and kept in a moderately heated room. In the early spring the old soil should be shaken from the roots and the plant potted into a big pot in good compost, and watered well.
Soon there will be other colours on the market.

Cephalocereus senilis (Old man cactus)

44   This is the heart-throb of all cactus collectors! However, it is a very difficult plant to grow. It is better for amateurs to start with less troublesome varieties before tackling this one. After some experience exciting results may be achieved with the Old man cactus. It is a very imposing plant, right from the seedling stage; it may grow very tall and will be covered in long white hairs, which are, in fact, modified hanging bristles. This cactus requires plenty of heat and flourishes in a heated room. However, it does not like dust because this becomes matted into the attractive hairs and is difficult to remove. This plant used to be imported but nowadays it is grown over here from seed. You may even order the seed yourself and when you have gained some experience with the easier varieties, achieve success. Sow in a pot with finely sifted and sandy soil, lightly cover the seeds, as they only need be just under the surface. Level the soil and cover with glass and paper. As soon as the young plants appear, remove both paper and glass, prick the seedlings out into another pot or box, and later plant each one separately in an individual pot. The plant requires a fine chalky soil. Repotting is best done during early spring. You can see from the sheen of the hair whether there is new growth and whether the correct repotting time has arrived. The plant may flower, but this is difficult to achieve in room conditions. Do not spray and water very infrequently during the winter.

Cereus peruvianus

45 A very old friend in the cactus family. There were, at one time, enormous specimens and even now one can sometimes see very large plants. In cacti exhibitions they are usually used as a background. They may reach a height of 10 feet and the stem may be up to 6 inches in diameter. They may flower, but not the indoor variety. This is not necessary anyway, as the cactus is quite attractive without flowers. It is one of the easiest varieties to grow and propagation can be done with seed or cuttings. Sowing seed is frequently done. You may do this as described with other varieties. Fill a pot with finely sieved sandy soil and only just cover the seeds. Cover the pot with a sheet of glass and paper. As soon as the young plants appear, remove both glass and paper. When the seedlings are well established prick them out and repot them each in a separate little pot. Later, when the plant is larger, a bigger pot is required. The plant does not need much water during the winter; once every three weeks is sufficient. During the summer watering can be done a little more liberally. There is also a fasciated variety of this cactus, which is a monstrous form in which the stems have run together. It needs the same treatment, should not be sprayed and can be propagated by cuttings, which can easily be removed from the fused stem.

No collection is complete without a specimen of this cactus.

Ceropegia linearis (Chinese lantern plant)

46   This is an extremely attractive trailing succulent, which one would not recognize as such at first glance. Small globules are formed in the axil of the marbled and fleshy leaves. You will find these also in the soil. As it is a true succulent, water only very sparingly during wintertime, once every two weeks is sufficient; during the summer this should be increased to once every other day. The long trailing stems have not only an abundance of globules but may also be covered with small lantern-shaped flowers. This really is a most attractive sight. It grows very easily as an indoor plant as long as the long stems have sufficient room to hang freely. It can stand the sun and needs no protection on a sill facing South. You may wish to give it some protection during the hottest part of the day, but the plant should be able to survive without it. Propagation is simple, take small pieces of the stem with globules on them and lay them in a small pot with sandy soil, where they will root rapidly. You will be able to delight your friends with this attractive little plant. It does not need much heat during the winter and a moderately heated room is sufficient for it. Older plants should be repotted during the spring. Use good quality potting compost. Do not forget the pieces of crock in the bottom of the pot and press the soil firmly into the pot. Regular manuring is essential for older plants as well as the cuttings. Use a well-known liquid house plant manure and apply it every other week.

Chamaecereus silvestrii (Gherkin cactus)

47   This is one of the prettiest of the smaller cacti and very popular in collections. It originates from West Argentina where it grows underneath bushes. This attractive variety produces short, cylindrical creeping branched stems which look like gherkins. It is very free flowering, usually in early spring. The bright red flowers are extremely beautiful. Despite ease of cultivation many people still fail with this plant and cannot get it to flower. This is due to incorrect treatment. If the plant is kept in a normally heated room it will develop very few flower buds, or will lose them prematurely. This pleasant little cactus does not require much heat during the winter but prefers a sunny place in an unheated but frost-free room. It needs only sporadic watering in these cool surroundings and the soil needs to be moistened only once every three weeks. If you treat it in this way and increase the watering in early spring, it will yield a rich crop of flowers.

Propagation by cuttings is very simple. When you touch the individual parts of the plant, they are easily disengaged and each separate unit can be cultivated. Do not use the normal potting compost as you can buy special cactus soil, which is readily available at any good nursery nowadays. During the summer months this cactus will do well on a window-sill facing East where it can have all the light and no strong sunlight. Facing South it should have a little protection.

Chamaedorea (Palm)

48   There are several indoor palm varieties but this is the best specimen for the living room, as it does not grow too high. This is an advantage if your space is rather limited. It requires slightly more heat than the other varieties, and should in any case be kept in a moderately heated room. It needs warmth as well as a very moist atmosphere. The plant likes to be sprayed regularly, which should be done with tepid water.

Chamaedorea can be propagated from seed. The seeds are thick and hard and do not germinate for a long time. They should be sown in a pot in a warm room, covered with a sheet of glass and paper. Keep the soil moist under the glass. When the young plants appear, remove both glass and paper. The small plants need protection against too strong sunlight. When the plants are well established, they can be repotted in individual pots in good potting compost. This plant needs plenty of water and it is advisable to mix the soil with a little heavy loam.

Generally speaking, palms prefer to grow in deep pots, rather than shallow ones. Give large plants a regular addition of manure, for which you can use normal liquid plant manure. Although many plants may be kept outside during the summer months, this variety should remain inside the house. Place it in such a position that the leaves are not touched. This palm may be plagued with aphids, but there are very efficient sprays available nowadays to deal with this complaint.

Chlorophytum comosum (Spider plant)

49   This is sometimes called 'Mother plant' but this is incorrect. Chlorophytum grows as a rosette-shaped plant. It has linear variegated white and green leaves. If you wish to keep these as attractive as possible, you should keep the plant in the lightest possible position but it cannot stand strong summer sun. You must provide some protection against it. This plant can flower, the flowers are white in colour and very insignificant and are borne on long thin stems. Keep the long stems after the flowers have died as within a short time many young plants will form on them. These can be removed later, complete with roots, and cultivated separately.

Chlorophytum is highly recommended for effective use indoors. If thick white roots show above the soil in the pot, you must repot the plant. Use a well known potting compost and do not forget the crock to cover up the hole in the bottom, which should never be blocked. The plant does not require much heat and will grow well in a slightly heated room. It must be watered freely and the soil in the pot must be kept damp. Weekly manuring is highly recommended and for this you can use a well known liquid house-plant manure. When removed from the pot the adult plant divides easily for purposes of propagation. The long, narrow, tapering leaves are very sensitive to handling and the plant should be placed where they cannot be touched.

Cissus antarctica (Kangaroo vine)

50 Cissus antarctica is better known as the Kangaroo vine. It is an excellent plant, a real climber which you will enjoy tremendously. It may cover an entire wall, but if things get out of hand, heavy pruning does not harm it in the slightest. It is best to do this in early spring. However, if your pictures are in danger in the autumn, the long shoots may be removed.

This plant thrives in a humid atmosphere and the leaves should be kept moist with daily spraying. If you do not wish the long shoots to be supported directly against the wall, you can erect a free-standing trellis, or hang a net, since its rapid growth will cover these quickly and enhance the decorative effect.

Cissus may be propagated by taking cuttings. This may be done at any time throughout the year. Young shoots, of approximately 4 inches, are placed in a jam jar filled with water and when sufficient roots have developed, each plant can be potted separately in nourishing potting compost. Cissus grows almost anywhere. If it is not too warm, it does extremely well in a living room, although if the atmosphere is too dry, it may shed its leaves. The best results are achieved in a moderately warm room. The soil in the pot should be kept well moistened. If the growth is insufficient, encouragement may be given by a little liquid manure every other week. The plant needs protection against strong sunlight but requires a light position. The florist usually supplies this plant in too small a pot, therefore repot fairly quickly.

Citrus japonica (Miniature orange tree)

51   This miniature orange tree comes from Japan. It can be cultivated indoors to grow fruits. They are quite large in size but are not edible. In May the fragrant orange blossom appears which has such romantic associations although the white flowers are rather small. If you want the plant to bear oranges, artificial cross pollination must be performed, removing the pollen of one flower to another by touching the open flowers with a small brush. Do not spray during flowering but later on a daily spraying will benefit the plant. The plant cannot stand too much heat and should therefore be kept in a very moderately heated room. Keep the soil in the pot very moist, as the plant has a great need for water. Fresh air is beneficial and for this reason the pot should be placed in front of an open window during the summer. It is a good idea to plunge the plant, complete with pot, in a light shady place in the garden until mid-October, when it must come back indoors. Sometimes a second flowering will occur during the late autumn, but these fruits will need nearly a year to mature. If there are any fruits left over from the May flowering, it is probably better to remove this new crop, as they will take too much of the strength of the plant. Feed regularly with a well-known liquid manure for indoor plants. Plants grown from pips can only be expected to fruit when they are pollinated by another plant. This can only be done by an expert. Perhaps there is a botanical garden nearby where someone would do it for you.
A new miniature variety from Florida can be cultivated as a house plant and will produce edible fruit.

Clerodendrum thomsonae (or var. balfouri)

52   The name Clerodendrum is derived from the Greek for 'chance' and 'tree' which probably refers to its variable medical qualities. It originates from West Africa and is very suitable for training up walls even though it can also be cultivated as a compact plant. The small flowers have pure white sepals which tend to change to pink and with a crimson corolla. They are extremely attractive and appear during the spring and summer so the flowering period is comparatively long and there is an abundance of flowers. It is not a very easy plant to cultivate, but once it has settled down, it will make an excellent show plant. It needs a light position but must be protected against the sun from mid-April to mid-September. After the flowering period yard-long trailing stems will develop. When these are well developed, they may need to be pruned slightly. An old plant must be well cut back and repotted after flowering. Use a well-known potting compost and press the soil well into the pot. The best place for this plant is a normally heated room, but it then needs frequent spraying which must be done with tepid water. The plant should be freely watered every day during its flowering period. The winter is a difficult time but the plant will survive if kept in a sunny place, especially when liquid manure is administered every other week. Propagation by making cuttings is possible but difficult to do in the house. You may try it after flowering.

Cleyera japonica

53 This plant is also known as Eurya japonica. With its tri-coloured leaves it is a most beautiful variety. This decorative plant is now mainly imported from Belgium. There are over eighty different species in this group, which occurs widely in South America and Asia. Only the specimen illustrated here is cultivated as a house plant, since other varieties may grow to enormous trees. The leathery leaves are attractively multi-coloured and should be sprayed regularly with tepid water. The soil in the pot should be kept moist. Do not forget that the ball of roots dehydrates more quickly than you realize. The plant should be kept in a moderately heated room.

Florists propagate this plant from cuttings. I have not seen many successful results from the attempts of amateurs at home, but you may try during the spring. Place a plastic bag over the pot containing the cuttings.

If repotting is required this can also be best performed during the early spring. Use a well-known potting compost and press the soil in firmly. Do not forget the crock in the bottom of the pot. The plant needs protection against the strongest sunlight, but on a window-sill facing East it will do extremely well and no protection is needed. Reduce the watering during the winter, when the plant should be kept in a frost-free but unheated room. It should then be possible to keep it alive until the next season.

Clivia

54 This plant is well-known and very popular, slightly old-fashioned, but still very charming. One frequently hears the complaint that it will not flower. This usually is because its resting period has been neglected. The Clivia must be rested during the winter and after mid-October manuring should cease and the supply of water be reduced. Watering on alternate weeks is sufficient, unless the plant is in the living room, when watering should take place once a week. However, the plant does not really like such a warm place and much prefers a moderately heated room. There are wide and narrow leaved specimens, the former ones are very beautiful with heavy clusters of flowers. During February the plant will form a flower bud and as the stem grows the water supply may be increased. When the stem is approximately 6 inches long weekly manuring should begin. Use a well-known liquid manure.

Clivias are subject to root-rotting; if the plant has been in the same pot for several years, it must be repotted. Shake the earth away from the roots and remove the rotten sections. Pot again with fresh potting compost. It is not necessary to increase the size of the pot, the one originally supplied is usually adequate for this plant.

Delay repotting until after flowering. Propagation from young shoots is quite simple: they form at the foot of the mother plant and can be removed when the plant is repotted.

Cocos (Syagrus) weddeliana (Palm)

55   This delicately leaved Coconut Palm is frequently used by florists for display purposes. It is a lovely evergreen house plant, first introduced during the late seventeenth century. It needs a fairly deep pot, which allows it plenty of room to grow. This is a very decorative plant which will greatly enhance your home if given proper care. The Palm can tolerate a great deal of water, so check whether the soil in the pot is moist enough. Other plants indicate whether they need water but with the Palm this is very difficult to see as the leaves will not go limp. With a continuous shortage of water, dry points will form at the leaf tips. They occur when the plant has been dry once and they do not disappear. Dry tips may also be caused by constant touching of the leaves. In this case the plant should be given more space.

Usually this plant is supplied in a pot which is too small and it is better to repot it straight away. Use good quality potting compost, and as the plant requires a heavy soil mixture, you can add some loam. Older plants cannot be repotted every spring, but you may keep them healthy by a weekly addition of a little liquid manure. The Palm likes a humid atmosphere. Spray frequently and keep the soil in the pot moist. Protection is needed against too bright sunshine.

Codiaeum (Croton)

56 These colourful indoor plants are better known by the name Croton. They are tropical evergreen shrubs which are extensively grown for their colourful ornamental foliage. The Croton may flower but the flowers are insignificant and as they retard the growth of the plant, it is much better to remove the buds early. There are long, wide leaved specimens, as well as varieties with very narrow leaves.

The Croton must be cultivated in a normally heated livingroom and requires full sunlight. The more sun it gets, the more exquisite the colouring of the foliage. No protection is needed on a window-sill facing East, on one facing South it is needed only on very hot days. The Croton also likes a humid atmosphere and the deep-dish method should be applied. Fill a deep dish with water, lower a saucer in it upside down until the bottom just emerges from the surface. Place a plant on this island, when it is then just above the water, but not in it. Daily spraying is essential and it is better to do this twice a day as the plant cannot stand a dry atmosphere. The soil in the pot should be kept moist and a weekly addition of a little manure is necessary. Propagation is by means of cuttings. Young shoots of about 4 inches will root in a small pot filled with sandy soil. Plants which have lost their leaves can be cut back in the spring and they can then be repotted in good potting compost.

Coleus

57 Coleus is a very pleasing indoor plant with colourful foliage. Coleus are particularly effective when used in flower arrangements, troughs or bowls in conjunction with grey foliage. They can be propagated by making cuttings and sowing seeds. Young shoots of approximately 3 inches root easily in a jam jar filled with water. When there are sufficient roots, each cutting can be potted into an individual pot or several cuttings can be put together in one pot.

Propagation by means of sowing is best done in the early spring. Do it indoors in a pot filled with finely sieved potting compost. The seeds are very fine and should therefore be covered over lightly; they only have to be just under the surface of the soil. Cover the pot with a sheet of glass and paper to prevent dehydration of the soil. As soon as the young plants appear, remove both glass and paper as the young plant needs the full sun at once. Later, prick them out and repot them and do not forget the smallest seedlings as they often produce the most beautifully coloured foliage. Finally, the young plants have to be repotted again into individual pots.

The Coleus requires frequent watering and a sunny position. During the summer it needs to be watered more than once a day. It also needs some liquid manure every week. This also prevents flowering, which is a good thing since the flowers are not attractive and they also weaken the plant.

Columnea

58　This is an evergreen trailing plant originating from tropical America. It is a profusely flowering specimen which needs careful attention. The scarlet or orange and scarlet flowers have a delicate beauty. You can see quite easily that this plant is related to the Gloxinia and so also needs protection against too strong sunlight. It will do well in a window facing East, but even then it needs a little protection from 10 o'clock in the morning. It requires abundant light and a normally heated room. As long as the plant is not in flower it needs to be sprayed frequently. Use tepid water, and under no circumstances cold tap water.

It can be propagated by means of cuttings. Always do this immediately after flowering and never before. Young shoots of approximately 4 inches long will root very quickly in a pot filled with sandy or peaty soil. In order to obtain a bushy appearance, put five cuttings into one pot. This is another plant which does well with the deep-dish method. Put some water in a dish and place a saucer upside down in it. The bottom should just emerge from the water and the plant is placed on it. The plant is now just above but not in the water. Reduce the amount of water during the winter and cease manuring altogether. Before the new growth starts in the spring, repot in a well-known potting compost to which a little extra peat-moss has been added.

Convallaria majalis (Lily of the Valley)

59   This well-known hardy herbaceous perennial loves a shady spot in the garden, where it flowers profusely in the early summer. Nowadays this attractive little plant can be bought, in flower, from a good florist or nurseryman at almost any time of the year. He is in a position to bring the flowering forward by placing the plant in a hothouse, or retard it by keeping it in a cool cellar.

You may flower Lily of the Valley in your own home in October or November. Plant one clump of a dozen or so single crowns in a 6 inch pot filled with well drained soil. Wet the roots thoroughly before planting and place the crowns with their long roots carefully and separately in the soil. The tip of the crown should be above the soil. After potting, keep the soil moist, cover the tips with moist peat-moss and keep it moist. Leave the pot in a heated room. When the tips grow through the moss, leave it in place for the time being to prevent dehydration of the soil in the pot. Later, when the plant is in flower, the moss can be removed but the soil must be kept moist. Lily of the valley requires light but not strong sunlight. After flowering the best thing you can do is to remove the plants from the pot and plant them in the open soil of the garden. They require a slightly shaded position and grow well at the foot of a shrub which is not too dense.

Cordyline (New Zealand Cabbage Tree)

60   At the moment the popularity of this beautiful, decorative plant is growing quickly and you should be able to buy it at many good florists. The reed-like leaves are reddish brown in colour with irregular bright red stripes. The plant requires a normally heated room as well as a humid atmosphere, so daily spraying with tepid water is essential and washing the leaves once weekly with a moist sponge is beneficial. The best method of cultivation is the deep-dish one: take a deep dish, place a saucer upside down in the centre and add water until the bottom of the saucer shows just above the water. Put the plant on this little island when it will be just above the water but not in it.

The Cordyline needs a weekly dose of manure. You can use the normal liquid house plant manure for this purpose. Use one teaspoon for 2 pints of water, this is sufficient for about twenty plants. This plant is attacked by aphids. If the weekly sponging of the leaves is not sufficient to deter them, you can buy some repellent spray which is very effective. This plant does not thrive very well in a crowded display trough and it should be carefully removed and planted separately. Use good potting compost and do not forget the crocks in the bottom of the pot.

Corytholoma (Gesneria)

61   This is a pleasant, profusely flowering plant which is becoming more and more popular. It belongs to the same family as Gloxinia and African Violet and for this reason it should also be cultivated in a normally heated room and it should be protected against strong sunlight. The scarlet flowers look very attractive against the dark green foliage but if the plant receives too much sun, the leaves will turn yellow.

Corytholoma is really a summer flowering plant but will continue to flower well into the autumn. After that it needs a rest. It is easy to keep it for planting again in the next season. Allow the plant to finish flowering and die back. When it has done this, place the plant complete with pot in a warm dry cupboard and you can forget about it during the winter months. In the early spring remove the dry globular root from the soil and plant it again in fresh potting compost. Do not forget to place the crocks in the bottom of the pot. At first keep the pot in a warm room and ensure that the soil remains relatively moist. Increase the watering when the young shoots begin to appear. When they are approximately 3 inches tall you must protect them against strong sunlight.

The plant needs frequent watering. A weekly addition of a little diluted liquid manure is beneficial. You must use a well known liquid house plant manure. Spraying with tepid water is good for the plant but it should be limited to the period when the plant is not in full flower.

Crassula falcata

62 This is a very attractive summer flowering succulent. The grey coloured leaves form a splendid contrast to the orange coloured flowers. Succulents usually do not require much water which is the reason why during the winter, when the plant is not growing, the soil should be kept fairly dry. Watering once every two weeks is sufficient. The plant can tolerate a good deal of sun but need some protection during the hottest part of the day. Propagation is easily achieved by taking cuttings since older plants form new shoots at the base. When these are approximately 4 inches in length, they can easily be removed and cultivated separately. Place the cuttings in the shade for a day to dry out. At the time of removal they are too full of water to root successfully. Plant them in a small pot filled with sandy soil. Repot later in a larger pot. You may use normal potting compost, but this succulent will grow extremely well in special cactus soil.

After flowering you may plunge the plant, complete with pot, in the garden. When there is a lot of rain, the attractive grey colour of the leaves will be temporarily lost. It may also be cultivated very well indoors.

It does not require much warmth in the winter, a slightly heated room is more than sufficient. Frequent watering is required during the summer, when it is also useful to apply a weekly dose of diluted liquid manure. Use a well-known liquid house plant manure.

Crassula lycopodioides (Shoe-lace plant)

63 Crassula lycopodioides comes from Cape Province. In appearance it resembles the old-fashioned shoe-lace, and it is known as such on the European continent. The square stems are covered on all sides with closely packed leaves, which lie on top of one another like roof-tiles.

This succulent is very popular and is grown frequently in bowls together with other cacti and succulents. Its main attraction is its peculiar manner of growing. The minute yellowish-white flowers are almost stemless on the stalk. The best soil to use is the special cactus soil as the plant does not grow well in normal potting compost. It does not require much watering during the winter (once every three weeks is ample). It needs a little more water during the summer, but even then twice a week is sufficient. The plant can tolerate a good deal of sunshine but needs some protection during the hottest part of the day. It does not require much heat and a moderately heated room is sufficient. Ensure that the position is sunny during the winter. If repotting is necessary, this is best done during early spring. Do not forget the crocks in the bottom of the pot. It is easily propagated by making cuttings or by division. Young cuttings will root easily in a small pot with sandy soil. Large adult plants can be removed from the pot and divided into pieces. If each section has retained some roots and young shoots, they will establish themselves quite easily.

Crocus

64 Indoor cultivation of crocuses is a pleasant hobby. There are many varieties and success can be met in various ways. Crocuses can best be grown in shallow pots or bowls. Put some compost in the bottom of the container and fill it up with ordinary garden soil. Put the bulbs close together so that they support one another. It is not necessary to place the bulbs in a dark cupboard first, but it is, of course, beneficial. In this case place them in a cool dark cupboard and keep the soil in the pot moist. Even better results are achieved if you first plunge the bowl in the garden, about 4 inches underneath the surface. Leave it there until the shoots are about 5 inches high, when the bowl can be placed in full daylight. However, they still should not have too much artificial heat. Only when the flowers begin to peep through the brown membranes can the bowl be placed in a warm room. Free watering is then essential. Even during flowering crocuses should not be placed in too warm a position or the flowering period will be shortened. You will enjoy them for several weeks if you keep them in an unheated, yet sunny and frost-free room. After flowering, the small bulbs are still useful. Remove the entire clump from the bowl and plant it in the garden. You can expect plenty of flowers for many springs to come.

Crossandra infundibuliformis

65 This is a pleasing little plant which is cultivated nowadays as a popular house plant. The salmon coloured flowers are closely spaced on the short spike and are its attractive feature. This small shrub was previously only cultivated in the hothouses of botanical gardens, yet it thrives very well in a normally heated room. You must supply it with a very humid atmosphere and therefore spray it frequently with tepid water. You can also give your little plant the deep-dish treatment. Take a dish, lower a saucer upside down in the centre and then add water in such a way that the bottom of the saucer penetrates the surface. Place the pot on the island when it will be above the water but not in it.

The plant may flower from early spring to late autumn. Keep the soil in the pot moist. Always use tepid water, because the plant cannot stand cold tap water. Propagation by means of cuttings is simple. Young shoots of approximately 3 inches will root easily in a small pot filled with sandy soil. They need repotting afterwards. Old plants which have over-wintered must be repotted in the early spring in good potting compost. At this time plants which have become too straggly can be pruned a little. The plant may shed some leaves during the winter, but do not worry, since they will soon be replaced during the spring. The plant cannot stand strong sunlight and must be protected from mid-April onwards.

Cryptanthus (Earth Star)

66   There are some hundreds of different species in the Bromeliad family but not many varieties are suitable for indoor cultivation because they occupy too much space on the window-sill. There are plants which do not grow so profusely and they belong mainly to the Cryptanthus genus. The name Cryptanthus is derived from the Greek words *krypto* (to hide) and *anthos* (flower). This is appropriate, as the flowers are insignificant and white and add nothing to the interest of this amazing plant. The leaves are hard and rather sharply toothed, but most strikingly coloured. This plant must be kept in a normally heated room and it also requires a moist atmosphere. It needs frequent spraying with tepid water. Never use cold water from the tap. This plant has very few roots and these grow close to the surface of the soil. It does not do so well in ordinary plant pots but prefers the shallow and wider variety. Moreover, there must be a good layer of broken crocks at the bottom of the pot. They really require a special soil mixture: chopped peat-moss and fern roots and half decomposed leaf-mould. This should be mixed with some silver sand and, if you can get it, rotted cow manure.

Older plants form side shoots at the base which can be removed easily when they are 2 or 4 inches high and then cultivated separately. Sometimes they separate from the mother plant of their own accord and only have to be potted. Protection against strong sunlight is necessary.

Cyclamen persicum (Sowbread)

67   Towards September the first specimens come onto the market and you will enjoy these splendid, prolifically flowering house-plants for several months to come. You should be able to retain the tuber until the next season, and start it off again. It is, of course, very tempting to buy a fully flowering plant, but it is much better policy to take one which has only a few flowers open but many buds to follow on. A normally heated room is not so good for the Cyclamen and it thrives much better in a very slightly heated room. It needs protection against strong sunlight but from mid-October onwards to mid-March it will tolerate all the sunshine it can get, and it needs a very light position. The florist will have supplied the plant with a good potting compost, but as you expect it to flower for a long time, some extra nourishment must be provided and it is useful to manure it a little every week. Cyclamen cannot stand cold tapwater. The water itself is obviously all right but the cold temperature can harm the roots. Add some hot water to make it tepid and water the soil in the pot. You may also add water to the saucer underneath but do not forget to remove any surplus water which has not been absorbed after a quarter of an hour as the plant cannot survive standing in cold water. It is possible to keep the plant for the following season but you must allow it a resting period after flowering. Repot the plant at the beginning of May in good potting compost and then plunge the plant and pot in the garden in a slightly shady place. As soon as the flower buds appear, take it back into the house.

Cyperus alternifolius (Umbrella Plant)

68   The name is quite apt, since the slightly bent dark green stems crowned with narrow leaves reminds one of an umbrella. In addition it is a plant which needs a lot of water. Complaints we receive about this plant are usually based on insufficient watering which causes dry leaf-points. The best method to overcome this is to place a bowl of water underneath the pot. Towards the evening you can throw the water away and in the morning renew the water again. The dry points also occur when the plant is in an atmosphere which is too dry. The leaves need to be moistened regularly. You may cut off the dead parts of the leaf very carefully with scissors. Leave a slight edge of the dead section otherwise the wound will create new dead parts.

The plant will tolerate plenty of heat. It thrives in a normal room temperature but considerable success may be achieved in slightly heated rooms. It can stand plenty of sun and protection is only needed during the hottest part of the day if the plant is exposed to the South. In a window facing East no protection is necessary.

Large plants may be divided in the early spring for propagation purposes and each section can be cultivated individually. Cuttings can also be taken. You need a leaf rosette with a stem of approximately one inch. Trim the leaf rosettes well and place them in a small pot filled with sandy soil. Keep the soil well moistened and place a plastic bag over the pot.

Cytisus racemosus (Broom)

69 Broom flowers profusely with yellow butterfly-like blooms. You can buy these attractive plants in the early spring from the florist and with little care and little artificial heat you can bring it to full flowering. A slightly warm room is more than sufficient to keep it in. Naturally it is much more exciting to buy a plant in full flower, but resist the temptation and chose one with only a few open flowers and many buds, you will enjoy it much longer. Keep the soil in the pot very moist, otherwise the numerous buds will shrivel; the root system dries out much quicker than you expect. A daily check of the dampened soil is well worth while.

This plant loves the sunshine but when it is in full flower it is better to give it a little protection, as the flowers will last longer. After flowering it is a good idea to prune the spreading branches a little. At this time repotting can also take place. Use the normal potting compost but mix a little sandy soil in with it.

The Broom can be plunged in the garden complete with pot during the second half of May, but you must give it a sunny position. Do not forget to water it and give it a weekly dose of manure. During the latter half of October the plant should be brought indoors again, at first in an unheated room, later it will appreciate a slightly warmer spot. Propagation is by means of cuttings made from the prunings removed during early spring. The cuttings must be placed under glass or underneath a plastic bag.

Dieffenbachia (Dumb Cane)

70 A very colourful decorative plant with leaves which are elliptical to heart-shaped and closely spotted and blotched on the upper surface. It is extremely popular in America but is becoming better known over here. Although not freely available there will be florists who stock this plant. You must not forget that this plant needs a very humid atmosphere and the deep-dish method is the only solution. Take a deep dish, lower a saucer upside down in the centre and add water until the bottom of the saucer just emerges from the water level. Place the plant on this small island; it is now just above the water but not in it. In addition, the leaves should be sprayed daily with a little tepid water. Keep the pot soil moist.

The Dumb Cane can tolerate some sunlight but it needs protection towards the end of April, otherwise the leaves will 'burn'. It requires a light place and during the winter it appreciates full sun. It can be grown in a normally heated room.

The plant will drop some of its leaves after a while, especially during the winter. When the stem becomes bare, you must cut it back severely, new shoots with beautiful leaves will form. Propagation by means of cuttings is possible but is better performed in a greenhouse. There are several varieties of the species. Dumb Cane is the best one and stronger than the others.

Dipladenia

71   One of the most modern house plants which was developed on a large scale only in 1959. It is a compact climbing plant, with dark pink buds which open as beautiful, rose-pink trumpet flowers. Not many florists will have them in stock, but they might be able to order one for you. It must be sprayed a good deal with tepid water and the plant can only be kept in a heated room. Usually it is supplied in a rather small pot and repotting will have to take place fairly quickly. This is best done during early spring. Use good potting compost and do not forget the crocks in the bottom of the pot as the drainage hole must not be blocked. It is a very pleasant plant which flowers nearly the whole year through. There will be not quite so many flowers during the winter but you can keep the plant going. This can be achieved by giving it a weekly small dose of liquid manure. The plant can tolerate quite a lot of sun. On a window-sill facing East no protection is needed, but this is not so for a window facing South. Propagation by cuttings is possible. Young shoots of approximately 4 inches must be put to root in a small pot filled with sandy soil. Later on they require a larger pot. If the plant produces too many shoots, you may trim it back a little during spring.

Dizygotheca elegantissima (False Aralia)

72   At first sight this plant does not look at all like an Aralia, but the finely divided leaves should give a clue to its status. This tender plant is really a hothouse shrub and should be kept warm in a normally heated room. It is best to use the so-called deep-dish method. Take a deep dish, turn a saucer upside down and lower it in the centre and then add water until the bottom of the saucer just penetrates the water level. Place the pot on this little island and the plant is now just above the water but not in it. The leaves should be sprayed regularly but you must use tepid water for this.

The florist uses this plant in displays and in bowls among other plants, but it is better suited for individual cultivation. It can withstand a good deal of sun but needs protection against strong sunlight. The plant needs plenty of water and on alternate weeks some diluted liquid house plant manure should be administered, the soil in the pot must be moistened beforehand. Sometimes this plant is attacked by woodlice. Touch the affected spot with a pencil dipped in methylated spirits and they will shrivel up. Repeat after one week.

Dracaena fragrans

73 This is a splendid decorative evergreen plant with handsome foliage. The leaves are fairly wide and have a broad cream or yellow coloured stripe along the margin. The plant needs a normally heated room and a very humid atmosphere. For this reason you should daily spray the leaves with some tepid water and the plant will greatly benefit by the deep-dish method. (A deep dish containing water and in the centre a saucer upside down just penetrating the water surface). Place the pot on this small island when the plant is just above but not in the water. Finally the leaves should be thoroughly sponged down every week.

The plant is fairly large and may require considerable space. It will look well in a bay window or on a wide window-sill. Usually the plants are supplied in normal sized pots but with continuous growth, these soon will be too small and repotting will be necessary. This may be done during the early spring. Use a well-known potting compost and do not forget to place the crock over the drainage hole which must not become blocked. From mid-April onwards, this plant should be protected against strong sunlight. If it is placed in too dark a position, it will lose its beautiful yellow colouring and it needs plenty of light to keep this. Old plants may be maintained by a weekly small dose of diluted liquid manure. For this purpose add one teaspoonful of the liquid house plant manure to two pints of water to make sufficient for about twenty plants.

Dracaena godseffiana

74 This is a completely different species of Dracaena, slender and rather widespread with numerous thin shoots. The leaves have yellow to greenish-yellow bright spots on them which remind one at first sight of Aucuba, but this plant is extremely different. Like the other Dracaena varieties it needs a very moist atmosphere and you will need to spray it with tepid water. It is also necessary to keep the pot soil quite moist. This small plant is often plagued with aphids and you must wipe the leaves down with a moist sponge every other week. Even though the other varieties cannot be propagated by division, this specimen takes to it very well. When the plant is well established it will have many shoots. If there are too many, you may remove the plant from the pot during early spring and divide it into pieces. Each section can be potted separately. Use a good potting compost and do not forget to place the broken crocks over the drainage hole in the bottom. The plant cannot stand strong sunlight and needs protection from mid-April to mid-September. If repotting is necessary, it can be done in the spring. Propagation from cuttings is also possible. Place the cuttings in a small pot filled with sandy soil in a heated room and put a plastic bag over it. Later the young plants can be repotted in a larger pot.

Dracaena sanderiana

75 This is an elegant decorative plant, however, as it has difficulty in developing side shoots it sometimes tends to look rather lanky. The foliage is very ornamental and rich in colouring. If the plant starts losing leaves at the base, it might be a good idea to plant it amongst other plants in a bowl. The plant is readily available in the shops. It should be placed in a normally heated room and requires a humid atmosphere. To provide this you may try the deep-dish method. Place a saucer upside down in a deep dish containing water so that the bottom of the saucer is just above the water level. Place the plant pot on this and the plant will be just above the water and not actually in it Spraying is very beneficial but tepid water should be used. Keep the soil in the pot fairly damp and when watering, also use tepid water.

The plant needs plenty of light but cannot stand strong sunlight and it needs protection from mid-April to mid-September. After this period you may place it in the full sunlight. It needs plenty of nourishment and should be manured once every week. You can use a well-known liquid manure for house plants. One teaspoon for two pints of water should make sufficient liquid to manure twenty plants. If repotting is necessary this can be done in early spring, using the normal potting compost. If water gets left in the leaf axils after watering it may be injurious to the plant so use the water very carefully.

Echeveria metallica

76 This is one of the best known Echeveria varieties – even in our grandmother's time it was greatly admired. It is conspicuous because of its pinkish-bronze leaves, which have a delicate white or reddish margin. It is an extremely popular houseplant often used in combination with other plants in a plant bowl.

Echeveria metallica needs full sunlight, even on a window-sill facing South it needs no protection at all. Watering can be reduced during the winter but it needs to be watered freely during the summer months: once a day is none too much during the summer, but this need be done only once a week during the winter. It does not need much warmth in the winter and it can be placed in a slightly heated room. It is not necessary to keep the plant indoors for the entire summer. It can be removed to the garden and planted or plunged in the open soil, with or without its pot. Choose a sheltered spot and do not forget to water it. The plant can be taken up in mid-October, leaving some earth on the root system, and potted again in potting compost and taken back indoors.

Propagation can take place by making cuttings. After a while there are sufficient young shoots at the base of the mother plant. When these are about 4 inches long they can be removed and planted in a small pot filled with sandy soil. They will root very quickly. Later they must be repotted in a larger pot. They require nutritious soil and cactus mixture (try a good nurseryman) is excellent for potting the cuttings in.

Echeveria setosa

77 This is a small species and a very attractive succulent which is easy to grow. They used to be grown exclusively for their colour effect in large flower displays but nowadays they are only grown as indoor plants. Succulents do not usually need a lot of water and a frequent error in keeping them is overwatering during the winter and underwatering during the summer months. Watering once every two weeks during the winter is sufficient but during the summer this has to be increased to once every other day.

This little plant does not require much warmth. It may be kept in a normally heated room but it prefers a slightly heated position. This is one of the reasons for the reduced need of water. Echeveria setosa flowers profusely and the bright red flowers with yellow tips make an attractive contrast to the grey coloured leaf. It is easy to propagate from cuttings. Older plants form neat small rosettes at the base, and when these are large enough you may remove them complete with roots and cultivate them separately with success.

Echeveria may be planted in the garden during the summer time and it looks very colourful in the rockery garden. When October comes the plant has to be taken up with the earth adhering to the root system, potted in cactus compost and placed in the moderately heated room. The sunnier the position, the more the plant likes it. No protection against strong sunlight is needed during the summer.

Echinocactus grusonii (Golden ball)

78 This is one of the oldest varieties of cultivated cactus and originates from Mexico. It is a very popular plant. It may become very old and large with an enormous globular stem decorated with long and attractive spines. This spherical cactus is easy to grow which is the reason why it is cultivated as a house plant and no cactus collection is complete without this interesting specimen. It can be propagated from seeds, which should be obtained in the early spring. Sow it in a pot with finely sieved sandy soil. The seeds should only just be covered. Place a sheet of glass and paper on top. As soon as the young plants appear, both glass and paper can be removed. When they become manageable, prick them out carefully and transplant them each into an individual little pot. Press the soil firmly around the plant as this is very important to all cacti. You can keep the plant in a fairly cool place during the winter and the watering can then be reduced. It is sufficient to moisten the soil with some tepid water once every month. The plant really prefers normal room temperatures, but in this position the watering must be increased. Do not expect it to flower as only very old plants produce flowers. These flowers are reddish yellow on the outside and yellow inside. If repotting is necessary, this can be done, as with other cacti varieties, during early spring. Young plants need a lot of water, especially during the summer months, but be very cautious with watering larger plants.

Echinopsis multiplex

79 This is a generally well-known cactus variety, appearing not only in cactus collections but also by itself on the window ledge amongst other plants. It grows easily and can be propagated quickly as it frequently develops many side shoots. There is a species which grows more erect, does not produce so many shoots, but flowers more easily. If propagation is required, this can simply be done by breaking off one of the many side shoots of Echinopsis multiplex. Leave the wound to dry out for a few days in the shade and then plant the shoot in a small flower pot filled with sandy soil. This variety should be given a little shade during the brightest hours of the day during spring and summer, otherwise excessive light will affect the colour. It can be propagated from seeds. This is done in early spring in a pot or pan filled with finely sieved sandy soil.

If repotting is necessary, this can also best be done during the early spring. Do not use normal potting compost if you can help it, but special cactus soil. The plant does not require much heat and a moderately heated room is sufficient. In such environment watering can be reduced to once a month. During the summer this should increase to every other day. It can be sprayed, but only during springtime when the new growth comes along and during the summer.

Episcia reptans (Cyrtodeira reptans)

80 This very attractive small plant comes from Colombia. It forms a ground level rosette of leaves which are beautifully coloured with roundish teeth. The variegated leaves combined with their red flowers make this plant very attractive. There is one variety with white flowers, but this is not so popular. This plant requires a humid heat and you will have to grow·it in a hothouse. Success may be achieved in the livingroom but you must then use the deep-dish method. Place a saucer upside down in a deep dish filled with water. Place the flower pot on the saucer which just emerges from the water. This makes the atmosphere around the plant much more humid. They develop thread-like shoots on the end of which young plants are formed. The short stalked hairy leaves should be sprayed regularly with tepid water. Give the plant the chance to be dry before the evening. Propagation is simply achieved by removing the young plants from the shoots and planting them in potting compost mixed with some moss peat. Do not forget the crock in the bottom of the pot and do not press the soil down as it should be aerated. Protection is needed from the sunlight from mid-March to mid-October. The plant requires additional nourishment and manuring once every fortnight is sufficient. Use diluted liquid manure and be careful not to spill any on the leaves.

Episcia dianthiflora with beautiful white flowers also makes a very pleasing house plant.

Erica gracilis (Heath)

81   Heaths are known by everyone and we can see many varieties cultivated in gardens. The real heather which grows wild is called Calluna vulgaris, but there is also the bell heather which flowers earlier. Nowadays there are heath and heather varieties which flower in the depth of winter. However, success is only guaranteed when the soil is poor in lime.

Heaths and Heathers are also grown as house plants. Erica gracilis is one of the most beautiful varieties and it reminds us of the wild heather. This plant flowers in November and December and you can enjoy it for a long time. Do not place the plant in the living room, as not only is the temperature too high, but the atmosphere is too dry. It must be placed in an unheated, frost-free room in a sunny position during the winter. Do not water with cold water straight from the tap in this cool situation. In any case, the plant prefers rain water which contains less lime, which no heather likes. You may manure it, but use only a small dose every fortnight. After flowering it is not easy to keep the plant. You can cut the plant back and possibly repot it, using the well-known heather soil mixture. During the summer it is best to plunge the Erica complete with pot in the garden in a place where it is protected from the midday sun. It should not stand under dripping trees either. Erica willmorei flowers in the early spring with flesh-coloured flowers. The treatment of this plant is the same.

Eucharis grandiflora (Amazon Lily)

82 Eucharis grandiflora is not very well known. It is a flowering, evergreen plant growing from a bulb. Although they are not readily available, you may be able to order them. When you decide to do this, order at least three bulbs as the plants prefer to grow close together and it is better to plant three bulbs in a wide pot than one in a small pot. Plant the bulbs in the early spring in very nutritious potting compost, mixed with a little heavy loam. The roots do not go down very deep and it is better to grow them in shallow pots or pans. Cover the bulbs over, and as they like both warmth and humidity it is even better to set the pots into a box containing peat-mould. Place a sheet of glass on the top and the soil in the pot will then remain much more moist. As soon as leaves appear, the glass should be removed. Cultivation is best achieved in a normally heated room. The beautiful white flowers, which have a very delicate perfume, may appear throughout the year. If they do, the leaves will require frequent spraying with tepid water. Do not expect as many flowers during the winter as the plant needs a rest. Watering can be reduced and no manure is necessary during that time. Scrape some of the top soil away in the early spring and place a fresh layer of potting compost on the top. Protection against strong sunlight is necessary.

Euonymus japonicus

83 There are many varieties of this much-branched, shrub-like house plant. The variety with variegated leaves of dark bright green with golden yellow are most sought after as indoor plants. It is an easy growing specimen, which does not require much warmth. It grows best in a moderately heated room, or even in an unheated one, as long as it is frost-free. During the summer it can be plunged in the garden, complete with pot, in a sunny position. Please do not forget to water it and spray frequently. The pot has to be lifted every week or so, otherwise the roots emerge from the bottom of the pot and get out of hand. During mid-October it is time to return the plant indoors to an unheated room but a light and sunny position is essential. If the plant is kept in a place which is too hot, it will be troubled by aphids. A spray against this pest can be bought.

Propagation by taking cuttings is very easy. It may be done during August Place young and vigorous shoots of approximately 4 inches long in a jam jar filled with water, to root. They can be potted afterwards, for which the normal potting compost should be used it possible with a little rotted oow manure. It is beneficial to give the plant a little diluted liquid manure from early spring to late September. Do this every two weeks and use a well-known brand of house plant manure.

Euonymus radicans var. fortunei

84   This is a bushy house plant with small silver and green leaves which are very attractive. It is a plant which will thrive under any circumstances except in a normally heated room, where not only is the temperature too high but the atmosphere is too dry. It can be kept in a moderately heated room or even in an unheated one, so long as it is frost-free. In a cool environment you will have to water it with tepid water. The little plant can be cultivated in the open soil of the garden, where it can remain as long as the winter is not very severe. For additional protection place some spruce branches over it. When planted in the garden, it looks very attractive against a low wall when the thin runners will hold on to the brickwork.

Propagation can be achieved by taking cuttings. Young shoots, approximately 3 inches long, will root very easily in a small pot filled with sandy soil. Later they may be repotted in a larger sized pot. Propagation of larger sized plants can also be done by division, removing the large plants from the pot and carefully dividing them.

This plant can stand a lot of sun and even during the summer it does not need any protection. Frequent spraying is essential during the winter if the plant is kept in a moderately heated room. Older plants will remain vigorous with a small dose of diluted liquid manure which should be given every other week.

Euphorbia fulgens (Spurge)

85   This is a profusely flowering house plant which is not cultivated very widely. Admittedly it is not a very easy plant to grow but with a little care and attention you may expect an abundance of flowers. The flowers develop during the winter months. The narrow leaves are elegant and orange flowers grow from their axils. The flowers are in fact insignificant, and the attraction of the inflorescence is in the coloured bracts. The plant needs plenty of sun, especially during the winter. The soil in the pot should be kept moist and not be watered with cold water, which is extremely harmful to the plant. You may also pour water into the saucer under the plant but if there is still some water left after a quarter of an hour, this should be removed.

After flowering the plant needs a resting period, when it may be put away in a cupboard, as the leaves will drop. In the early spring you will have to nurse it back to life. Remove the plant from the pot, shake the old and dry soil away from between the roots and plant it again in new potting compost. Prune the long branches to a length of 12 inches. The plant should then be placed in a sunny position in a normally heated room. During the summer you may plunge it, complete with pot, in the garden. Do not forget to water it and return it to the house before October. Propagation can be achieved by taking cuttings in the early spring from the young shoots which appear.

Euphorbia milii (Crown of thorns)

86 This plant has some resemblance to a cactus in its shape and spines, but it is a true succulent. This can be seen when the plant is damaged and a white liquid, which is rather poisonous, emerges. Be careful that you do not get this in an open wound.

This succulent, which flowers profusely, should be placed in a sunny position in a slightly heated room. The normally heated room is really a little too warm. It may flower for the major part of the year and the small red flowers are very attractive. Sometimes the plant suddenly loses all its green leaves which turn yellow and drop. Do not worry about this, it is the plant's way of asking for a resting period. Stop manuring and water very infrequently. A six weeks' rest works wonders and after that you will notice the formation of green buds which will develop into small leaves. Watering can be increased again and manuring begin. If repotting is required it is best to do it when the new growth starts. Use normal potting compost and do not forget the broken crock in the bottom of the pot. Special cactus soil is excellent. It can be propagated by making cuttings. Young shoots of approximately 4 inches can be made to root in a small pot containing sandy soil. Watering must be done with tepid water, you can use the ordinary tap water but add some hot water to it.

Euphorbia pulcherrima (Poinsettia)

87 Around Christmas Poinsettias are available in abundance as cut flowers. The plant is also very popular as a house plant. It must be placed in a normally heated room but not near a fire or a radiator as it cannot stand dry heat. The plant hates cold tapwater, which should be mixed with some hot water to make it tepid. After some weeks the beautiful red bracts will drop, the green leaves turn yellow and one is left with a bare stem. The plant can be very easily kept until the next season. When the plant is bare of leaves, it should be put away dry in a cupboard. Around mid-April you remove the plant from the pot and cut back the stem to 4 inches. Shake off all the dry, stale earth from the root system and repot the plant in good potting compost. Do not forget the broken crock at the bottom of the pot. The plant should then be placed in a warm room and must have full sunshine during summer and winter. After some time new shoots will appear. Leave two for each plant and remove the others. During May the plant can be put in the garden, complete with pot, in a sheltered and sunny place. Do not forget the watering and weekly manuring. The pot should be lifted and turned to avoid roots growing out of the pot. At the end of September or the beginning of October it should be returned indoors, at first to an unheated room, and later to a warmer room.

Exacum affine

88   This is a sweet little plant with delightful bluish-lilac flowers. It is a true summer flowering plant. It can be propagated by sowing seed during early spring. This can be done indoors in a flowerpot and the seeds should only just be covered. After sowing the pot should be covered by a sheet of glass and paper. Keep the soil moist and as soon as the young plants appear both glass and paper must be removed, because the seedlings need direct sunlight. When they can be handled they should be pricked out and replanted at an inch apart in a small box. As soon as the leaves touch one another, it is time to plant each seedling into its own individual pot, using normal potting compost. At this stage the plants would benefit from a stay in a greenhouse. Later they should be repotted again into a larger pot.

When the plant is in full flower you can take it into the living-room and place it in a sunny position. A little protection is needed during the hottest part of the day. It needs a lot of nourishment and should be given a weekly dose of diluted liquid manure. It is possible to keep this plant for the next season, but the care and attention involved are considerable for the poor results achieved. It is much better to sow afresh in the spring or to buy a flowering plant in the summer. Generally speaking, this plant thrives better in a dry living room than in the humid hothouse of the nurseryman.

Fatshedera (Climbing Figleaf Palm)

89   This is another plant with an unfamiliar Latin name. The plant is a hybrid and its name is derived from Fatsia or Figleaf Palm and Hedera or Ivy. The leaves are smaller than the Fatsia but larger than the Ivy. It is an easy growing house plant. It can be drastically pruned if the plant grows too high. Plants can only become bushy if the plant is cut back regularly. This can be done during the spring or during the summer. The young shoots can be used as cuttings. If you place these when they are approximately 4 inches long into a jam jar filled with water, they will root easily. It is not necessary to use tip-cuttings, even parts of the stem provided they have leaves will root in water. The plant is usually supplied in a small pot, which makes it necessary to repot it fairly quickly. Use the normal potting compost and do not forget to place a piece of crock in the bottom of the pot. The Fatshedera flowers, but only when the plant is a few years old.
The plant likes plenty of nourishment, and a little diluted liquid manure may be administered once every fortnight. It likes a lot of water and the soil in the pot should be kept moist. The plant needs protection against bright sunlight, but it requires a light position, preferably on a window-sill facing North. The plant prefers a slightly heated room and a normally heated room is too much for it. The variety with a variegated leaf needs more warmth.

Fatsia japonica (Figleaf Palm or Japanese Aralia)

90   This popular evergreen house plant is much better known by its English name 'Figleaf Palm'. There are varieties with green and silver blotched leaves. The green-leaved sort requires little warmth and can be cultivated in an unheated but frost-free room. The variety with the variegated leaves needs a moderately heated room.

The green-leaved is so hardy that it can be planted in the open soil in the garden. Find a sheltered spot and plant it during mid-April but not much later in the spring. At the beginning of the winter you will have to place a reed mat around it and cover the top with some spruce branches. If the winter is not too severe to start with, it may well withstand the cold weather very well.

Do not keep the plant in high temperatures, the leaves will turn yellow and drop. They may grow very tall and wide and require a lot of space. Propagation by taking cuttings is easy, place young roots of approximately 6 inches in a pot filled with sandy soil, they will then root. If the plant grows too tall, aerial layering may be a solution. Make a length-wise shallow cut into the stem at the desired height. Wrap peat around the stem and the plant will develop roots. When this has taken place cut the plant underneath the moss and plant the top part. You will then have a lovely new plant.

Ficus diversifolia

91   This is a very special member of the family of Ficus. It is grown mainly for its small fig-like fruits which are not edible. The plant is as yet rather difficult to buy.

It is a shrub-like plant, which requires very little room since it usually does not grow more than 10 inches high, nor does it become very wide. It is best to cultivate it in a moderately heated room, since normal room temperatures are too hot for this plant. It requires a humid atmosphere and needs spraying regularly, for which tepid water should be used. The soil in the pot should be kept moist. As with all other Ficus varieties, the plant is very susceptible to cold water. The watering should therefore be done with tepid water. The plant needs quite a lot of sun it will do fine in front of a window facing East, but facing South some protection is needed during the hottest part of the day. Repotting is best done during early spring. Branches which have outgrown their strength should be pruned a little. If it is not repotted, a weekly small dose of diluted liquid manure is called for.

Propagation by taking cuttings is easy and should be done in early spring. Young shoots of approximately 3 inches can be taken. Place them in a small pot with sandy soil and cover it over with a plastic bag.

Ficus elastica var. decora (Rubber plant)

92   There are quite a few pitfalls in growing the rubber plant. One is that the leaves droop rather easily but this is caused by the wrong watering treatment. First of all, this plant cannot stand cold water. You may use tapwater for watering purposes, but add some hot water until the temperature is tepid. If you prefer watering on the saucer, the surplus water should be removed after a quarter of an hour, or the water which is left will be too cold, and will harm the plant. Do not leave any water in a decorative overpot, since it will cause brown spots on the leaves. Leaves may droop or die if the soil in the pot is too dry, so a daily check is called for. Many diseases can be avoided if the plant is placed in a warm enough room as it needs warm surroundings.

The plant needs a weekly dose of diluted liquid manure. Use the normal liquid house plant manure. If the Ficus grows too tall, aerial layering will solve the problem and give you another plant. Make a shallow cut in vertical direction in the stem between two leaves. A milky liquid will appear. Wrap the cut with moist peat-moss which is protected on the outside with a plastic bag. Keep the moss moist inside the bag. The plant will form roots in the moss and the top part can be cut off just below the moss. The new plant has to be potted in potting compost. It is also possible to make cuttings. The plant needs protection against strong sunlight. The variegated leaved plant should be grown at a higher temperature.

Ficus lyrata (Fiddle-leaved fig)

93   A very decorative plant with large violin-shaped leaves. It is very popular in the United States but for some unknown reason not often seen in British homes. The plant may become overpowering in a small room as it grows both tall and wide. However, the plant can be kept under control by aerial layering. Make a shallow, lengthwise cut in the stem between two leaves. Wrap moist peat-moss around it and a plastic bag on the outside. Keep the moss moist. After several months – life in the living room is slow moving for a Ficus – roots will be formed. When they appear on the outside of the moss, the plant can be cut off below the moss patch. Pot the top part in good quality potting compost and you have a new plant. Keep the old plant a little longer because it will form new shoots, which can be removed and will root easliy in a fairly large jar filled with water. Later they can be planted.

Ficus lyrata should be cultivated in a normally heated room. It requires a very humid atmosphere and the leaves should be kept moist by daily sponging with tepid water. Older plants should be kept healthy by regular dosing with manure. Use a well-known liquid house plant manure. The plant can stand the sun, but it needs protection from mid-April to mid-October from strong sunlight. It thrives in a light position and will do well in a garden room.

Ficus pumila (Creeping fig)

94   Sometimes this variety is sold under the name Ficus stipulata or Ficus repens. It is a beautiful plant which you will enjoy for years. The plant can be grown both as a creeper or a hanging plant. It requires a humid atmosphere and it is therefore beneficial to spray the small leaves daily using tepid water. Ficus pumila can be propagated by taking cuttings. Young shoots of approximately 3 inches will root fairly easily in a small pot with sandy soil. You can also place the cuttings in a jam jar filled with water where they will root quite happily. When they have sufficient roots, each cutting can be potted separately in a small pot and cultivated normally. After some years the Ficus can grow very wide and the narrow leaves look decorative against the wall. If you wish you can fix a net which will provide sufficient support for the plant to grow up. Eventually it may take up too much space but then severe pruning will prove a solution. The plant needs nourishment and a small dose of liquid manure every other week is necessary. The plant is usually supplied in a small pot and it will need to be repotted very quickly. You must use good potting compost for this. The plant likes plenty of light and sun in the early spring, autumn and winter. In the summer it needs protection against too strong sunlight. This Ficus variety is popular in mixed plant bowls. After a while you may remove it from there and cultivate it separately.

Fittonia

95 This attractive, prostrate creeping plant is named after Elizabeth and Sara Mary Fitton, the authors of *Conversations in Botany*. It is a delight to see in any normally heated room. The leaves are egg-shaped, bright green and beautifully netted with white veins. The variety shown here is easy to grow, even though it requires a very moist atmosphere and should be sprayed daily on the leaves with tepid water. Do not use water straight from the tap. The roots of this dwarf plant do not go down far into the soil and it more or less creeps over the surface. For this reason use shallow wide flower pots. If you have only deep pots fill them with broken crocks till halfway up the pot. The plant requires a well aerated but nutritious soil mixture. Use the normal potting compost to which is added a good quantity of peat-mould. Fittonias can be propagated by taking cuttings. This is best done during early spring or summer. Young shoots of approximately 3 inches root fairly easily in sandy soil. The plant cannot endure strong sunlight and it will need protection from mid-March to mid-October. It will shed some leaves during the winter but this is not harmful to it. It needs repotting in the early spring and then new leaves will grow. There are some varieties with red-veined leaves, these do not grow very fast and are not so suitable for home growing. Fittonias may flower but the small yellow flowers are rather insignificant.

Fragaria indica (Strawberry)

96 This is a low perennial herb with red fruits which are not edible. It is very old-fashioned, first introduced in the seventeenth century, and it is usually grown as a hanging plant. It produces small white flowers, which are followed later in the summer or autumn by red fruits. Cultivation is fairly simple as it does not require much warmth. It may even be possible, during a mild winter, to keep the plant in the garden in the open ground. It then needs some protection with spruce branches. However, it is much better to keep the plant indoors for the winter. Place it in a light position in an unheated but frost-free room. It does not need much watering during winter. It can be propagated by sowing seed in the early spring in a pot indoors, but in the autumn the plant produces long thin shoots which bear young plants. These can be removed complete with roots and planted. During the growing period the plant needs to be watered freely and the soil in the pot must be kept moist. Give it a small dose of diluted liquid manure every other week. Ten years ago this plant had vanished altogether, but now it is growing in popularity, mainly for its attractive little fruits. The plant can be trained around an iron hoop. Repotting of old plants is not necessary, because there will be plenty of young ones. If you wish to do so, it must be done in the early spring. Use normal potting compost.

Fuchsia

97 The Fuchsia is a rather old-fashioned plant which has suddenly come to the fore-
ground again. They can be grown both indoors as well as in the garden. One of the complaints about this plant is that it sheds open flowers and flower buds but this can be
prevented by plunging the plant in the garden after mid-May. Place the plant in its pot
in a position which is slightly shady during the hottest part of the day.

There are many varieties and colours, both with double and single flowers. Propagation
is easily achieved by means of cuttings. Young shoots of approximately 3 inches may be
placed in a jam jar filled with water to root. When there are sufficient roots they may then
be planted separately in small pots with good potting compost. Press the soil firmly
round the plant. Later the seedling has to be repotted into a larger pot. Fuchsias may be
kept indoors during the summer. They will do well on a window-sill facing East where
they do not need any protection. They need enormous quantities of water and a weekly
dose of diluted liquid manure. After mid-October the plant needs a rest and it has to be
kept indoors, and manuring should cease. It can be cut back and left for the winter in an
unheated but frost-free room. Repot early in the spring and prune a little more. You may
train the Fuchsia to grow into a wide plant but then the centre has to be taken out of
young shoots. If you want the stem to develop, then this type of pruning should not
be done.

Gardenia jasminoides (Cape Jasmine)

98 During the twentieth century the Gardenia family has met much competition from other well-known cutting flowers. This is the reason why they are no longer so popular as they used to be. Yet occasionally very attractive house plants can be seen. The difficulty in growing them lies in the fact that the buds tend to drop off. If you increase the manuring during the bud formation, the strongest buds will develop, but the weaker ones will drop. This shedding of buds may also be encouraged by climatic conditions, by insufficient watering, or the sudden drying out of the soil in the pot. The temperature in the room should be kept at the same level both day and night. Even though they may sometimes be made to flower right throughout the year, you should consider yourself extremely fortunate if your gardenia flowers in spring and autumn.

The plant requires a moderately heated room and the atmosphere should be sufficiently humid. This may be achieved by frequent spraying with tepid water. This plant would do well with the deep-dish method. Lower a saucer upside down into the centre of a water-filled dish. The bottom of the saucer should be just above the water level. A plant placed on this is just above the water and not in it. The Gardenia needs a heavy soil mixture and normal potting compost should be mixed with some heavy loam. Do not forget the broken crock in the bottom of the pot. Early protection is needed against strong sunlight, although the plant likes a light position. When there are no flower buds, weekly manuring is beneficial. The success of cuttings is dependent on soil temperature and is difficult to do under normal circumstances in the house.

Gloriosa (Climbing Lily)

99　Gloriosa is also called Climbing Lily. It is a fine flowerer which needs plenty of space. It can be kept for years since the tuberous roots last a long time. Order them very early in spring from a reliable firm as they may be rather difficult to obtain. When the tubers arrive, plant them three to a pot. The pot should be quite large and so-called crysanthemum-pots are the best. Place a layer of broken crocks in the bottom of the pot and fill only half the pot with good quality potting compost. Plant the tubers in this in such a way that they are just below the surface and keep the pot in a warm room with the soil moist. Thin shoots will appear and when these reach a height of approximately 8 inches, fill the pot to the top, very carefully, with potting compost. Be careful not to damage the tender shoots, otherwise you will not have any flowers.

The beautiful red-yellow flowers are very lily-like. If too many of them develop the plant may have to be supported by small sticks in the pot since the thin stems are not strong enough to carry the weight of the flowers. The plant requires full sunlight and frequent spraying. After flowering the plant may be left to die back gradually, after which the pot can be placed in a cupboard and you may forget about it all during the winter. In the early spring remove all the stale and dry soil and repot again in fresh potting compost.

Grevillea robusta (Silky oak)

100 Grevillea robusta, which is more generally known as the Silky oak, makes an attractive pot plant. It is 2 feet or more tall, with dark green feathery evergreen leaves, which are silky on the undersides. It does not often flower. The plant does not require much warmth and a normally heated room is too warm for it. During the summer months it can be plunged in the garden, complete with pot, where it should be kept in a sheltered and sunny position. The pot should be turned and lifted every week, otherwise too many roots will be produced and will grow out of the bottom and over the top of the pot.

Give the plant plenty of water. The plant is usually supplied in a pot which is too small, so repotting should take place very soon. Use the normal potting compost and do not forget the crocks at the bottom of the pot.

Grevillea robusta can be propagated by taking cuttings; young shoots of 3 to 4 inches long will root fairly easily in a small pot with sandy soil. However, the Silky oak can also be grown from seed and it would be fun to try this. Fill a pot with finely sieved potting compost, sow the seeds, cover the pot with a sheet of glass and paper and place it in a warm room. When the seedlings appear, remove both paper and glass as the young plants need the full light at once. Later you may plant the seedlings in small pots and when they grow bigger, repot them again into a larger pot.

Guzmania (Bromeliad)

101 The genus Guzmania contains some of the most beautiful of the Bromeliads and many which are suitable for room cultivation. The plant is from Peru and requires a warm temperature, so it must be grown in a normally heated room. As it also requires a very moist atmosphere, it should be sprayed frequently or even better grown by the deep-dish method. Place a saucer upside down in a deep dish containing water, in such a way that it penetrates the water level. When the plant pot is placed on the saucer, the plant will be just above the water but not in it and the atmosphere around it will be more humid. Protection against strong sunlight is essential but the plant likes a light position. No protection is needed on a window-sill facing East.

This Bromeliad flowers only once and after that the young side shoots must be cultivated. At the base of the mother plant young shoots develop regularly after flowering. When these are 4 to 6 inches in length, they can be removed very carefully together with their roots. They may be cultivated separately, but do not use the normal potting compost. Use a mixture of chopped peat-moss and Osmunda fibre, beech leaf-mould and some sharp sand. Do not forget the crocks in the bottom of the pot. It is useful to cover the soil in the pot with some peat-moss which should be kept moist.

Gynura aurantiaca

102 This splendid evergreen plant comes from Java. It has impressive ornamental purple tinted leaves and is becoming more and more popular. The leaves have small purple hairs on both sides and are the main attraction although it may bear clusters of small yellow flowers.

The easiest way to grow this plant is from cuttings. Cuttings removed from the centre of the plant may be used for this purpose, but the side shoots are also very effective. They need considerable warmth and should be placed in a warm room with a plastic bag over them. When the cuttings have sufficient roots they can be planted separately in small pots filled with good quality potting compost. During the summer repotting to a larger pot will be required. Do not forget the crocks at the bottom of the pot. The plant should be protected against strong sunlight but no protection is needed on a window-sill facing East. It also needs a humid atmosphere and frequent spraying is necessary. Do the spraying early enough in the day to leave the plant enough time to dry before the night. The plant should be watered freely, keeping the soil in the pot moist. A weekly dose of diluted liquid manure will benefit the plant. During the winter the plant should be kept in a normally heated room. You will have to take cuttings very frequently, as the older plants tend to grow too tall and straggly. The younger plants are more beautifully coloured; the old leaves turn green and lose their attractive purple colour.

Hedera helix (Ivy)

103   This well-known plant can be grown as a trailer or a climber. It can be grown outside
in the garden but it is also very suitable for indoor cultivation. The florist will nearly always
supply this plant in a pot which is far too small and repotting will be necessary. The plant
does not require a high temperature and a normally heated room is really a little too much
for this plant. The plant flourishes in an unheated but frost-free room. In these cool
surroundings do not forget to water with tepid water and spraying is very beneficial to it.
The plant should be placed in a light spot but protection against strong sunlight is
necessary. Propagation by taking cuttings is fairly easy to achieve. Young shoots of
approximately 4 inches long will root easily in a jam-jar filled with water. Later they can
be potted in a small pot filled with a good quality potting compost.
There are several varieties and those with gold and silver coloured leaves are
extremely attractive. In some varieties these coloured leaves are very small while in others
they are fairly large. The large shaped leaved variety is not so easy to grow, it requires
more warmth and should be grown in a normally heated room. The variegated plants need
protection against the sun. The plant is sometimes troubled by aphids and a protective
spray against this kind of pest can now be purchased readily in any good seedshop.
A small dose of diluted liquid manure every fortnight will be very beneficial. The green-
leaved variety can be plunged in the garden complete with pot during the summer
months. This should be in a light but shady position.

Helleborus hybrids (Hellebore, Christmas Rose)

104 There are only a few species in the Helleborus family from which all the others have been derived by crossing. The best known is the white Christmas rose, Helleborus niger, which flowers around Christmas. As long as these are not placed in an atmosphere which is too dry or too warm, you will enjoy them for a long time. The plants may also be cultivated in the open in the garden but they then need a very rich soil, so mix the garden soil with rotted cow manure (if possible) and heavy loam. Place them in a light, shady position, such as at the base of a medium-sized shrub. Towards the end of November the plants are sometimes already covered in flower buds. The plant can then be removed from the garden, planted in a wide pot and placed indoors. Until the flower-buds have opened, daily spraying with tepid water is necessary. The soil in the pot must be kept moist. After flowering in the early spring, the plant can go back to the garden, again in the open soil. A variety of Christmas rose with bronze-purple flowers can also be used as a garden plant and has approximately the same requirements as the white variety. It flowers only during the early spring. It is a very attractive indoor plant, but should not be in too warm a position: a sunny place in a frost-free, unheated room is ideal. After flowering you may remove this plant to the garden. The colour-range between these two varieties is enormous, but they need the same treatment. They can be propagated by means of division of the plant after flowering and each section can be planted separately.

Hibiscus rosa-sinensis (Rose of China)

105   This is a plant which is very well known to people who have been in the tropics. It is a deciduous flowering shrub and in the East it is covered with lovely flowers for the best part of the year. In this country it is grown very successfully as an indoor plant. Originally there were only varieties with red and pink flowers but new varieties are now available with yellow and white and double or single flowers can be seen. The double flowered variety is particularly popular. The large flowers are often only open for one day, but as there are so many of them, this does not matter very much. Please do not forget that the plant should be placed in a normally heated room and requires a very humid atmosphere. Frequent spraying of the leaves with tepid water is essential. Although the plant requires some sunlight, it needs protection on a window-sill facing South. The plant should be watered freely so keep the soil in the pot well wetted and use tepid water.

Hibiscus needs a lot of nourishment and a weekly dose of diluted liquid manure is essential. Use a well-known liquid manure for indoor plants. It can be propagated by taking cuttings. Young shoots of approximately 3 inches long can be placed in a jam jar filled with water, where they will root easily. Afterwards they can be potted. In the early spring, the plants which have been kept over the winter should be heavily pruned and repotted. Use a normal good quality potting compost which has been enriched if you can with a little rotted cow manure.

Hippeastrum hybrid (Amaryllis)

106 Amaryllis used to be quite popular as a cut flower but nowadays it is becoming very popular as a house plant. However, if you wish to have an Amaryllis for indoor cultivation, order a Hippeastrum: the true Amaryllis is a bulbous plant suitable for the garden. There are many splendid colours available, the orange-red or white varieties are very impressive, but the pink and salmon-pink flowers are extremely attractive. You should order the bulbs from a reliable firm in October, and they should be potted at once in good potting compost mixed with some rotted cow manure if you can get it. Dot not forget the crocks at the bottom of the pot, and place the bulb two thirds above the soil in the pot and only one third beneath. The best position for the pot is a warm mantelpiece. At first the plant does not need much watering, but when the flower-bud appears, watering should increase. When the flower stem is approximately 12 inches high, the plant should be placed on a window-sill facing South. The leaves should have developed by then. After flowering the flower stem should be removed and the plant will need a weekly dose of diluted liquid manure. After mid-May the plant can be plunged in the garden, complete witn pot. At first it needs nutritious soil which will encourage the roots to penetrate the bottom of the pot and grow over the top. Do not forget to water it and give it its weekly dose of manure. Stop watering in mid-August and leave the plant to die back slowly. Afterwards it can be removed to a dry cupboard, and as soon as the new flower-bud appears the plant should be repotted.

Hoya bella (Small Wax flower)

107 Hoya bella is a very attractive house plant. It is not very well known yet, which is a pity, because it is much prettier than the large Wax-flower. It is a recumbent plant from India, which can be grown as a hanging plant. The flower clusters are much smaller than with the large Wax-flower, but there are large numbers of them and they smell very sweetly. The plant requires a moderately heated room but can be kept in the living room. However, as the atmosphere is usually rather dry there, regular spraying is essential, using tepid water. It is really a kind of succulent, therefore it is sufficient to keep the soil in the pot only slightly damp.

It is necessary to keep the Hoya bella in more or less the same place. It is most frequently cultivated as a hanging plant and if it is moved often it will drop its flower buds. If the pot is placed in a window-sill, you should mark the front of the pot so that it will be put back in the same position after removal.

Propagation of the Hoya bella is done by taking cuttings. This should never be done before flowering; wait till immediately afterwards. Young shoots will root easily in a small pot filled with sandy soil. If you want a nice bushy plant, you should place five plants in a wide pot. The plant must have a regular dose of a well-known diluted liquid manure. Manuring should stop when the flower buds are forming, as if the plant grows too vigorously, it will drop the flower buds.

Hoya carnosa (Wax-flower)

108   The Wax-flower from Australia is better known as a house plant than Hoya bella, it is more suited as a climbing plant and you can guide the long trailers along a hoop of wire, which reduces the space it requires. People sometimes complain about the flower buds dropping. This is caused when the plant is moved too frequently. If you make a mark at the front of the pot, you will always be able to put the plant back in exactly the same position as before. The best results are achieved if this Hoya is grown on a window-sill facing East, the changes in temperature are not so great there and no protection is needed. When placed on a window-sill facing South, the plant will have to be protected during the summer. The large clusters of pleasant smelling, waxy flowers develop in abundance, but when the buds form you should stop manuring, otherwise the growth becomes too vigorous and the buds will drop. Daily spraying with tepid water is beneficial. Leave the dead flowers on the plant as new flower-buds will develop where they occur.

Propagation of the Wax-flower can be achieved from cuttings, which should, preferably, be taken immediately after flowering. Young shoots of approximately 4 inches long should be rooted and then placed in a small pot filled with sandy soil. Older plants should be maintained by a weekly dose of liquid manure, using a well-known house plant manure.

Hyacinthus (Hyacinth)

109 It is easy to grow early-flowering Hyacinths, and it is fascinating to watch them progress, especially if they are grown in water. You can buy special Hyacinth glasses with which success is assured. Order your bulbs in September from a reliable firm. For water culture you not only need the early flowering variety, but bulbs which have been specially prepared by subjecting them to treatment which enables them to flower about Christmas. Fill the glass with tap water and place the bulb in the top section; the bulb should be just a little above the surface of the water. Place the glass in a cool dark cupboard and replenish the water when necessary. If you tip the glass a little, filling is easier. When the glass is filled with thick white roots and the tip of the bulb is about 3 inches high, the plant may be taken into the warm room. After flowering these specially treated bulbs should be thrown away as they are useless.

Hyacinths can also be brought forward by planting them in pots filled with soil or bulb fibre. They first have to be dug, complete with pot, into the garden and placed 6 inches below ground level. When the tops are 3 inches high they may be removed to the warm living room. The soil in the pot should be kept moist. There are many colours and varieties; the white and red ones are especially popular, but the blue, pink and yellow ones are also very lovely. When the bulbs are in full flower they should be removed to a cooler position.

Hydrangea

110   Hydrangeas are very popular as indoor plants. They can be kept in a moderately warm room and after flowering removed to the open soil of the garden. Treated in this way you can expect beautiful large flowers for years to come. There are also blue Hydrangeas but this colour is induced by the florist. He dissolves a little aluminium sulphate in the water used for watering and red and pink Hydrangeas become blue coloured. You can have the same colour change if the soil in the garden contains iron. It is therefore possible that your pink Hydrangea may change into the blue form a few years after transplanting into your garden.

In the early spring and summer the florist will have a large selection of this attractive plant. Your Hydrangea should be watered freely and put in a light position. Some protection from sunlight is required, otherwise the large flowers will droop. After flowering the plant can be cut back to just over an inch above the old growth. The difference between the old and new growth can easily be seen, the young wood is still green and the old wood brown. When you transplant the plant then into the garden, allow plenty of space because the small house plant may grow into a sizeable or even enormous shrub. A distance of approximately 3 feet apart is desirable. Propagation can take place from cuttings. These should be taken immediately after flowering, as the young shoots develop after pruning.

Hypocyrta strigillosa

111 Hypocyrta is from Brazil, and is an up-and-coming house plant which bears abundant flowers. If it is grown in a small pot, it develops into a bushy, compact shrub which can be kept in a moderately heated room. The soil in the pot should be kept moist as the plant easily dries out. In winter it requires some warmth, a light position and care must be taken not to over-water it. It is easy to propagate this plant by taking cuttings which can be done immediately after flowering. Young shoots of approximately 3 inches will root in a small pot filled with sandy soil. When they are well established, their tops have to be pinched out a few times to make bushy plants, and they will also require larger pots. Use the normal potting compost to which a little fine sand should be added. This plant will also grow well from seed, but this is best done in a greenhouse during early spring. During the summer months the plant may be plunged in the garden, complete with pot, but it has to be taken indoors after mid-October. During the summer and in the early spring a small weekly dose of diluted liquid manure is very beneficial. The plant can stand full sunshine, but it has to be watered. Old plants which have been kept over the winter can be propagated by division, which is best done during the spring.

Hypoëstes sanguinolenta

112   This is a plant with beautiful foliage which originates in Madagascar and is very suitable for indoor cultivation. Its leaves are dark green, mottled white and have fiery red veins. The flowers are lilac with a white throat and dark purple markings, but are less attractive than the leaves. This plant is a good grower and may reach a height of up to 20 inches. It sometimes becomes a little bare of leaves at the base and it is better to nip out the centres a few times; the new, branched stems will then make it into a well-developed bushy plant. Older plants have to be pruned frequently and new cuttings have to be taken, otherwise growth becomes too straggly.

Cuttings are best made during the spring, when overgrown plants have to be cut back. Ample growths, approximately 3 inches long, will be available for rooting in small pots filled with potting compost. Place them in a heated room. At first protection is needed against strong sunlight. Older plants also need protection against the sun during the summer, but not if they are on a window sill facing East. This plant requires much warmth and should be kept in a normally heated room. It also needs plenty of light and a very humid atmosphere. Frequent spraying is essential and tepid water should be used. The soil in the pot should be damp. The old overwintered plants can be repotted in the early spring, using the normal potting compost. Do not forget the crock in the bottom of the pot.

Impatiens (Busy Lizzy, Balsam)

113 Impatiens is much better known as Busy Lizzy. This fast growing many-flowered house plant will be a delight in your house from early spring to late autumn. It may even flower during the winter. There are beautiful colours available nowadays, the orange variety in particular is very pleasant. Originally a water plant, its demands for water are enormous. The best solution is to place the plant on or in a saucer filled with water. This should be refilled daily, but any water left in the saucer at night time should be removed. Spraying is also beneficial. The plant flourishes in a normally heated room but also does very well in a slightly warm room. Place the pot in a very sunny place, as if its position is too dark, the plant will drop its flower buds. This will also occur if the atmosphere is too dry.

It is easily propagated from cuttings, as young shoots will root in a jam jar filled with water. When they have sufficient roots they can be potted in a small pot, using normal compost. It may lose some leaves during the winter, and the overwintered plants should be cut back heavily during early spring and then repotted. Use potting compost and do not forget the crocks at the bottom of the pot. Old plants will retain their strength if given a weekly dose of diluted liquid manure. It is also possible to plunge the plant, complete with pot, in the garden during the summer months.

Ipomoea (Morning Glory)

114   There are many varieties of this plant, of which rubro-caerulea is most noteworthy. The flowers open purple, mature sky-blue and are very attractive. This plant can be grown from seed which should be sown in the early spring. Order your seed early from a reliable dealer and sow indoors in a medium sized pot filled with sandy soil. The rather large seeds should be placed about $\frac{1}{2}$ inch under the surface of the soil and no deeper. Place the pot in a warm room and cover it with a sheet of glass and paper, keeping the soil moist. As soon as the seedlings appear. remove both glass and paper as the young plants require light As they should really be sown singly in a pot in which they can mature, you should not sow many seeds in one pot as the seedlings do not transplant easily. Surplus seedlings should be removed, leaving about 4 of them to a wide pot, to produce rapidly as it were one fully grown, bushy plant. This climber produces an abundance of flowers but it requires a sunny position and needs frequent spraying with tepid water. Small stakes should be placed in the pot to which the tondrils may attach themselves. Large plants need a lot of water and a weekly dose of diluted liquid manure. This plant is not perennial and must be sown each spring.

Iresine herbstii (Achyranthes verschaffeltii)

115   This very attractive house plant was first introduced during the mid-nineteenth century, and was used almost universally as a decorative foliage plant in formal bedding in parks. They are still used for this purpose, especially in the Canary Islands, where they combine them with other plants and make bell-shapes.

The brilliantly coloured, wine-red leaves are exquisite. The plant can be the centrepiece of your display trough if kept in a warm room. Warmth and regular spraying are essential. Use tepid water also for watering which should be done frequently. It is propagated by taking cuttings of young shoots approximately 3 inches long. These can be made to root in a jam jar filled with water, and when sufficient roots have developed, each plant can be potted separately into a small pot filled with a good quality potting compost. Later the plant should be repotted in a larger pot. The plant may flower, but the flowers are insignificant. Pinch off points of shoots frequently to induce bushy growth. The plant can stand full sunshine and even on a window sill facing South no protection is required. If repotting is necessary, this is best done during early spring when plants which have grown too straggly should also be cut back hard. The tops may be used as cuttings. During the summer the plant may be plunged in the garden, complete with pot, but it should be taken back indoors by mid-October when the weather becomes too cold for it. You may also plant them out in the open in the garden but only after mid-May and up to mid-October. These plants could be the result of the cuttings you have taken.

Iris reticulata

116   This early flowering bulbous perennial grows well in the garden, as well as indoors. If you want to grow them outside, order bulbs in August. They should be planted 4 inches deep and 4 inches apart in good soil, in which some compost or rotted manure has been mixed. If the winter is mild, you can expect them to flower in mid-February in your garden. They look best when planted in the front in the border. To grow them indoors they should be planted in a bowl or pot, perhaps 10 bulbs close together. So fill the bowl with ordinary garden soil that the bulbs can be covered with 2 inches of soil. The pots should be plunged in the garden and covered with 4 inches of garden soil. Towards the end of January the pot will be ready to be taken indoors, at first to a slightly warm room. Keep the soil in the pot moist and do not use liquid manure. After flowering the irises can be planted out in the open garden, where they should flower again the following year. There are a number of coloured varieties, either purple or blue, or variations of these colours.

Ixora

117   People who have been in the tropics will know this flowering evergreen bushy shrub. The large red or orange coloured flowers are reminiscent of the Hydrangea, but not nearly as big. In Holland they are frequently grown as house plants. The fragrant flowers develop mainly during the late summer and are known for their beauty. However, this is not an easy plant to grow and is one which definitely needs the deep-dish method. A saucer is placed upside down in a deep dish containing water (the bottom of the saucer should be just above the water level). Place the plant on this and it will be just above the water but not in it. When the living room is very warm during the winter, it is essential that the leaves should also be sprayed with tepid water. When the plant has finished flowering, it will need a rest of approximately 6 weeks. The watering can be reduced and no manure should be given during this period, but the spraying should continue. In the early spring the plant can be cut back slightly and repotted at the same time. Use a good potting compost and do not forget the crocks at the bottom of the pot.
The plant needs plenty of sun during the winter and the early spring, but after mid-April some protection is needed. Older plants will keep their strength by a small weekly addition of diluted liquid manure. Use a well-known brand. Ixoras are often used by florists in combination with other plants to make up plant bowls.

Jasminum (Jasmine, Jessamine)

118   There are many species of this plant. The winter flowering Jasminum nudiflorum is very successful in the garden, where the bright yellow flowers are most attractive. There are also some species which can be grown as house plants or in a greenhouse. Jasminum sambac originally came from India and Indonesia and is one of the best known of them. Jasminum gracillimum is a climber with finely divided green leaves, which also makes quite a pretty house plant. The white flowers are very lovely.

The species used as house plants should be grown in a light but not too sunny room. The plant should produce an abundance of their very fragrant flowers. If the long shoots become too unruly after flowering, they can be cut back, as this will not harm the plant at all. If necessary, the plant can be repotted at the same time. Use a well-known potting compost and do not forget the crocks at the bottom of the pot, as the small drainage hole should not become blocked up. Growth will stop during the winter and the plant may drop some leaves. However, during the spring new growth will appear and soon the plant will be covered with its white flowers once again. It is easy to propagate from cuttings; this is best done during early spring. The plant can stand a fair amount of sun but needs some protection during the hottest part of the day. The soil in the pot should be kept moist and frequent spraying is necessary. Do not forget to give it liquid manure, which should be done once every fortnight during spring and summer.

Kalanchoe

119   An attractive succulent plant which may flower throughout the entire winter. The small flowers are garnet-red or orange-red. This plant can be made to flower as early as the autumn but you must then apply the 'short-day-method'. Florists use this method, because the flowers do not normally appear until early spring. In their country of origin, the plants are influenced by the shorter period of daylight and form flower buds more readily there. To achieve this artificially, place the Kalanchoe for three weeks during August in the dark from 6 at night to 8 the following morning. You will be amazed at the result. This small plant is very modest in its requirements for space. A normally heated room is too hot for it so place it in a slightly warm room for preference. It need not be watered so frequently there, as long as the soil in the pot is kept moist. If the plant is overwatered, the erect stems will rot and the plant will die.

After flowering the plant can be cut back and should be repotted, using good potting compost. During mid-May the plant can be plunged in a sunny position in the garden, complete with pot. The plant can be propagated from cuttings, which are best taken during the spring. After cutting back there will be sufficient shoots which can be used as cuttings. The cuttings will root easily in small pots containing sandy soil, later they must be repotted in larger pots.

Lampranthus blandus (Afternoon flower)

120   This plant, sometimes known as Afternoon flower, is often included under Mesembryanthemum. This succulent produces an abundance of flowers which are very beautiful.
There are many varieties of this plant which have different coloured flowers, for example
Mesembryanthemum blandum roseum, which produces large pink flowers. There are also
varieties with white or salmon-pink flowers. Success can only be achieved if the plant is
placed in a sunny position since it requires full sunshine, not only during the winter but
also during the summer.

During the winter the plant does not need much warmth and a slightly warm room is more
than sufficient for it. During this period watering can be reduced but it should be increased
again during the summer, when watering once a day is essential. The propagation of this
plant is by means of cuttings. This may be done in the spring, summer or even autumn.
Young shoots of approximately 3 inches long should be put in a small pot filled with
sandy soil when they will root easily. If you wish to have a bushy plant which flowers well,
in the shortest time, you should place perhaps 7 cuttings in a normal sized flower pot.
During the summer the plant can be plunged in the garden, complete with pot, in a sunny
position. Planted in open soil in the rockery, the plant will flourish, but sufficient cuttings
must be taken before the temperature drops below freezing point. If you wish to repot
older plants, this can best be done during early spring. Use the special cactus soil, which
can be bought in a seed shop.

Lantana camara

121   If you visit Italy during the summer you will be impressed by this plant in full flower. It is a shrubby plant with tawny orange flowers. Nowadays the colour range includes other colours, of which the lilac variety is extremely attractive. The plant is easy to grow, it does not require much warmth and can be kept during the winter in a slightly warm room.

Plants are still not readily available over here, but you may be able to order one at a good flower shop. If your window-sill becomes overcrowded during the summer, the plant can be removed to the garden, where it can be plunged in the ground complete with pot, in a sunny position. If you keep the plant indoors on a window-sill facing South, then it needs some protection. The plant can be propagated from cuttings, which should be taken in early spring. An old plant may drop a fair number of leaves during the winter. You may cut it back heavily and use the young tops as cuttings. Placed in a small pot with sandy soil, they will soon root. Later the young plants have to be repotted into a larger pot. Use good potting compost and do not forget the crocks at the bottom of the pot. They need a lot of nourishment and a weekly dose of liquid manure is necessary from early spring to late autumn. Plants have been crossed and various combinations of colours are now to be seen. If the tips of the growths are removed you will get a bushy plant but you can also grow this plant with a well-developed central stem. In this case do not remove the tips of the growths but let the main stem grow up straight.

Lithops (Pebble Plants)

122 Lithops are small succulents originating in South Africa. They grow in dry desert country. They sometimes grow entirely below the surface of the sand, where they are protected to some extent from the fierce sunlight. They have adopted the shape and colouring of the pebbles amongst which they grow possibly as protection against wild animals which would eat a visible plant. They flower during the rainy season, when a little more nourishment is available. There are differently coloured varieties and the flowers are extremely attractive. However, flowers should not be expected with room cultivation. At the top of the thick, nearly spherical leaves is an area through which the plant absorbs light, even when nearly covered over by sand.

Careful cultivation is not necessary with this plant: it grows vigorously in a sunny position in a room. The more sun the better, and a place on a window-sill facing South is called for. Use cactus soil in the pot. The plants can be grown in small pots, preferably shallow ones or bowls. The soil in the pot should be kept only moderately moist and during the winter it is sufficient to water only once a month. Lithops require a moderately heated room. The plant can be grown from seed, when available. Sow in a pot indoors, in a warm room.

Mammillaria

123   These plants are relatively easy to grow. There are many cacti which are known as Mammillaria, although experts sometimes sub-divide them into other families. The plant is not only attractive when in flower, but its form of growth makes it pleasant to look at, even when there are no flowers to admire. They do not like too much artificial heat and prefer to be placed in a slightly warm room. Be careful with watering in these cool surroundings; once every three weeks during the winter is ample. You can moisten the soil in the pot with a small amount of water but the plant should not be sprayed. When the spines become more colourful in the spring, you may rightly assume that the new growth has begun and watering may then be gradually increased. When the plant begins to grow really well, it may be lightly sprayed during the day. Cacti may be watered more freely during the summer but once every other day is sufficient.

The plant can be grown from seed, which should be sown in a pot filled with finely sieved potting compost. The fine seeds should only be just beneath the surface of the soil. The pot should be covered with a sheet of glass and paper and put in a warm room. As soon as the young plants appear, both may be removed. Young plants have to be pricked out several times; later each small plant can be potted separately into a small pot. Use cactus soil which you can often buy at a seedsman's. The plant needs protection against strong sunlight.

Maranta leuconeura var. kerchoveana (Ten commandment plant)

124   This is an attractive, well-known, ornamental house plant which you will enjoy for years. The oval leaves, held more or less horizontally, are pale green, bearing 10 fine chocolate-brown blotches on each side of the midrib, hence the American common name. This plant does flower in the house but the small white flowers are insignificant and its main artistic value lies in the strikingly beautiful leaves. The plant needs protection from strong sunlight from the beginning of March. It should be grown in a normally heated room and needs a very humid atmosphere. If the air is too dry, the leaves will develop dead tips and once this occurs the decorative value of the plant is lost. The leaves should be sprayed daily with tepid water and the soil in the pot should be kept damp. Propagation is best done by division of the plant, which can be carried out in the early spring. Remove the plant from the pot and divide it into sections. Cut off all the old leaves, especially leaves with dead edges, and repot the plant in fresh potting compost. Maranta does not like a deep pot, and does better in a shallow one. If you do not have one, you can fill a deep pot one third full with broken crocks.

The plant likes some manure, especially during spring and summer, and it will benefit from a small weekly dose of liquid manure until late autumn. Use a well-known brand of house plant manure. The other variety shown here, Tricolor, has beautiful colourful leaves.

Medinilla magnifica

125   This tropical plant comes from Java and the Philippines. When it is grown as a house plant, it needs a very humid atmosphere, so frequent spraying is essential. Be careful to see that the undersides of the leaves are also sprayed regularly. This plant should really be cultivated by the deep-dish method. Turn a saucer upside down and lower it into a deep dish filled with water until the bottom of the saucer just emerges. Place the pot on this artificial island. The plant is now just above the water but not in it. This plant can be freely watered with tepid water. The soil in the pot should be kept very damp, especially at growing time and when flowers start to appear. The plant needs plenty of space as it may reach a height of 5 feet and its width is also considerable. Flowering occurs during the summer or autumn. The real flowers are small and insignificant, but the hanging flower clusters are enveloped by pink bracts which give the plant its elegant appearance. Raise the pot off the window-sill when the plant is in flower, otherwise the clusters will touch the pot or the window-sill. After flowering, which is usually during the autumn, a resting period is required. Manuring should cease and watering be reduced. If necessary the plant can be repotted after the resting period and plants which have grown too straggly may be cut back a little. A nutritious but well-aerated soil is required, so mix the potting compost with a little sandy peat. There must be sufficient crocks at the bottom of the pot. The plant needs protection against strong sunlight and should be grown in a very warm room.

Miltonia (Pansy-orchid)

126   Orchids occur in almost every part of the world, but in the tropics there is a greater variety of them with the most beautiful flowers. In the past they all had to be imported, but this is no longer necessary as conditions for propagation have been well developed. Miltonia is sometimes known as Pansy-orchid because of its appearance. There are two main groups.

The first group is derived from mainly Colombian species which grow high up in the mountains and should therefore be cultivated at fairly low temperatures. The other group is of Brazilian origin and therefore requires more warmth. Many beautiful hybrids have been raised. Miltonia spectabilis and its descendants will grow particularly well as house plants. A normally heated room is a little too warm for this plant, it prefers only a slightly warm room. It is essential to use rain water and not tap water for watering. Orchids need a special soil mixture which may be bought ready mixed, but if you have bought a flowering plant from a florist, it is better to ask him to do the repotting when necessary. Repotting should take place every other year, preferably just before the growing period, in any case after flowering. It is essential to protect the plant against too strong sunlight. No spraying is necessary, except on hot days. Keep the soil in the pot moderately damp. There are also many other orchids which can be grown as house plants.

Monstera deliciosa (Swiss cheese plant)

127   There are few more magnificent sights than this tropical evergreen plant which you will enjoy for years. It starts its life as a normal pot plant but develops into an impressive climber. If it grows too high, the main stem can be cut back to encourage the plant to develop side shoots and to reduce its height. The top can be used as a cutting and this new plant should grow very well, especially if it has some aerial roots which may be used as ground roots.

This plant requires a light but very nutritious soil, so use normal potting compost mixed with a little leaf-mould, and when possible well rotted cow manure. Older plants develop aerial roots which should not be cut off. The plant requires a very moist atmosphere and quite a lot of warmth, it must therefore be grown in a normally heated room. The soil in the pot should be kept damp and the water used for watering must be lukewarm. Daily spraying is necessary, for which tepid water must also be used. The plant requires a lot of feeding and a weekly small dose of diluted liquid manure is useful. Direct sunlight is detrimental to the plant and after mid-March it must have some protection. Generally, young plants show only deep incisions in their leaves and it is only with the older leaves that holes appear. The plant can produce its extraordinary cream coloured flowers, which are followed by an edible fruit resembling a pineapple in flavour.

Narcissus

128 This spring flowering bulb can be cultivated to flower earlier indoors. The paper-white variety in particular is extremely suitable for this and does not even need soil. Paperwhites can be planted in a shallow dish with pebbles and water. Order the bulbs from a reliable firm, place some gravel on the bottom of the dish, plant the bulbs on the gravel in such a way that they slightly support one another. Fill the bowl with pebbles and water. The dish can be placed straight away in broad daylight in a very moderately heated room. The dish must be watered regularly and the pebbles should not be allowed to dry out. Once the Narcissi flower, keep them in a cool room and they will last for a long time. After flowering the bulbs are useless for forced flowering and they will not flower in the garden either, so they should be thrown away.

Other Narcissi can also be grown to flower in pots, but they do require a period inside a dark cupboard. It is also possible to plunge the pots in the garden and cover them with approximately 4 inches of soil. When the shoots are approximately 4 inches high, they can be taken indoors into the warm room, where they require a lot of water. If the pot of bulbs is kept in a dark cupboard, success is equally assured and the bulbs should be kept there until the shoots are about 4 inches high. Yellow trumpet daffodils are extremely suitable for this type of cultivation and white cluster narcissi can also be used with great success. For early flowering you will need pre-treated bulbs.

Nephrolepis (Fern)

129   This is a very well-known type of fern. It is an elegant and very decorative house plant which you will enjoy greatly. Nearly all ferns require a humid atmosphere and this one is no exception. It should be placed in a normally heated room or even a slightly warm one. It also requires frequent spraying which should preferably be done in the morning because the curled leaves should be dry towards the evening.

You should have great success with Nephrolepis but as the florist usually supplies this plant in a pot which is too small, repotting should take place fairly soon. Use normal potting compost mixed with some peat-mould and rotted cow manure as the plants need a very rich well-aerated soil. Do not forget the crock at the bottom of the pot. Large pots cannot be repotted every spring, so the nutriment in the soil must be maintained by a weekly small dose of diluted liquid manure. Use a well-known house plant manure. During the winter months manuring can be greatly reduced but the plant should still be watered regularly. The plant needs to be watered freely during the summer months and also to be protected against strong sunlight.

Propagation is not difficult by division, which is best done during the spring. Large plants can be removed from the pots and divided, and each section may be grown on individually. The attractive leaves can be used as a decorative background for cut flowers.

Nerium oleander (Oleander)

130 You may have seen Oleanders in full flower in Southern Europe. You may even have taken some cuttings, planted them here at home and have come to the conclusion that the plant just would not flower. However, they can be persuaded to flower if you do not forget that the plant must be kept in the full sunshine. The tightly closed flower buds will only open when they are exposed to the full sunshine and if they are sprayed regularly with tepid water. It frequently happens that the Oleander is grown at much too high a temperature and the plant cannot stand artificial warmth to this extent. It should be kept frost-free during the winter months and a very moderately heated room is sufficient. The plant needs plenty of water if it is kept in a sunny position; watering only once daily is not sufficient and this should be increased to twice daily. Spraying is essential, not only of the flower buds but also of the leaves. After Mid-May the plant can be plunged in the garden, complete with pot. Give it a sunny position and plenty of water. Early in October the plant should be returned indoors. It can stand a fair amount of manure, but this should not be added after the flowering buds have formed.
Propagation by cuttings is verry successful; young shoots of approximately 6 inches long will root easily when placed in a jam jar filled with water. Later they can be potted in small pots filled with potting compost. There are varieties with pink, white and also red flowers.

Nertera granadensis (depressa) (Bead plant)

131   If it were not for its orange berries, this small plant would be insignificant. The leaves are minute and the tiny green and white flowers hardly noticeable. However, after flowering the appearance of the orange berries guarantees several months of enjoyment. The roots of the Bead plant do not penetrate the soil very deeply, so cultivation in a shallow pot is therefore recommended. You may be able to buy these shallow pots at the seedshop. If your plant is in a medium-sized flower pot, the pot should be one third full of broken crocks. The plant needs a normally heated room but can also be grown in a moderately heated one. It requires a humid atmosphere, but it should not be sprayed since this affects the small leaves, which will rot. The deep-dish method is much more suitable. Lower a saucer upside down in a deep dish containing water. The bottom of the saucer should be just above the water level and the plant placed on this artificial island. The plant is now just above the water but not actually in it. The air around the plant is now much more humid. The plant needs protection from direct sun, when growth is active it should have a little diluted liquid manure once every fortnight.
It can be propagated by division of the plant in the early spring. The soil should be composed of potting compost with some leaf-mould and sharp sand.

Notocactus leninghausii

132 This cactus is very popular amongst amateur plant growers, not only for its beautiful flowers, but also for its attractive spines. The spines are golden yellow and extremely fine. The flowers which appear at the top of the plant are about 2 inches long, the outer petals being greenish and the inner ones yellow. It is not easy to make it flower under room conditions, but even without flowers the plant is still attractive. This cactus is grown from seed, which should be sown in April (you can order the seed at a seed shop). Fill the pot with finely sieved, sandy soil and scatter the seeds. Do not cover the seeds too much, as they should be only just beneath the surface of the soil. After sowing, the seeds should be covered over with a pane of glass and paper. As soon as the young plants appear, both glass and paper should be removed as the seedlings need the sun. As soon as they can be handled, they should be pricked out in a bowl or pan, at a distance of approximately 1 inch apart. Use cactus soil which you can buy at a seed shop. Later the plant needs protection from direct sun. It can be grown in a normally heated room. Watering as well as spraying have to be reduced during the winter. It is sufficient to moisten the soil in the pot approximately once a month.

Odontoglossum grande (Orchid)

133 Growing and nursing orchids is an absorbing job, but some experience is essential. If one is successful with handling other difficult plants, good results with orchids are not impossible. There are many varieties but most of them are only suitable for hot-house cultivation. However, this variety can be grown in room temperatures in a very moderately heated place and sometimes it flourishes even better than in the humid and warm hot-houses of the professional grower. Odontoglossum forms its flower buds in September, which is the best time to order the plant. It is well worthwhile visiting specialist orchid growers.

A plant with flower buds showing will give pleasure straight away. For the time being leave it in an unheated room and when the outside temperature drops, put it in a slightly heated room. The plant needs protection from direct sunlight at least until mid-October. Spraying with tepid water is beneficial, but for this it is best to use rainwater. Keep the pot soil a little less moist after flowering and, if necessary, repot in the spring. Do not use the normal potting compost. The soil should consist of peat and osmunda fibre, mixed, if possible, with some half-decayed beech leaf-mould. Do not forget to place a layer of broken crocks in the bottom of the pot. The brownish yellow flowers are extremely beautiful and you will enjoy them for weeks on end. No manuring is required.

Opuntia

134 The cultivation of cacti is a satisfying hobby. Some people have extensive collections and there are even societies of amateur cacti growers who publish their own journal. There is an enormous variety of cacti, many of which can be grown with great success as indoor plants. The Opuntia genus is a large one and there are some very beautiful species. One of these is Opuntia ficus-indica which is shown here. The joints of the stem are large and smooth, the spines are almost absent. It can become very tall so you will need space, but it will take years before the plant reaches such a size that it becomes awkward and then cuttings can be taken.

Opuntia ficus-indica does produce yellow flowers, but only when the plants are quite old. This variety, as well as others, does not need much water or heat during the winter. Generally speaking, they prefer a slightly warm room even though the plant requires a sunny position. It is sufficient to water the cactus once every three weeks during the winter months, but during the summer it should be done every other day. In a cool place the water used must be lukewarm. Propagation by means of cuttings is simple since every full grown section can be broken off without any difficulty and will root easily in a pot containing sandy soil. To begin with the watering of new cuttings should be limited. There are other species with very attractive variegated spines, these usually do not grow so high and are therefore extremely suitable for room cultivation.

Pandanus veitchii (Screw Pine)

135   The variegated screw pines are well liked as decorative plants and very suitable for indoor cultivation. There are many species, this one comes from Polynesia and is one of the easiest to grow. It requires normal room temperatures and should be sprayed a good deal. Use tepid water as cold water from the tap will harm the plant. The soil in the pot should be kept moist. The variegated leaves narrow to a long point and have a sharp cutting edge, so the plant must be placed in a position where it cannot be touched easily. When the plant becomes a little older, it develops aerial roots. They are quite substantial and can be put in the soil of the pot and in this way support the rather weak stem of the plant. In its natural state in the tropics, the plant uses these aerial roots as anchorage and the stem may then degenerate altogether. The aerial roots should not be cut away.

The easiest way of propagation is by means of the young shoots, which appear in numbers at the base of the old plant. When these reach a height of approximately 6 inches, they can be removed, complete with roots, from the mother plant. They can then be grown separately, using normal potting compost, but mix it with some peat-moss as the plant likes a nutritious, well aerated soil. The plant may reach a fair size and plenty of space should be allowed. There are other varieties which are not so suitable for room cultivation.

Paphiopedilum (Venus' slipper)

136   In the past orchids were always grown in hothouses. Nowadays many varieties can be grown as house plants. One of the most suitable and also the best known is this Paphiopedilum of which there are many different species. One of the best known ones is Paphiopedilum insigne, which flowers during the winter months. The best time to buy the plant is in the late autumn when they have flower buds. You may have to order such a plant from an orchid grower. This orchid does not require much warmth; it prefers a very moderately heated room to the humid atmosphere and the high temperature of the hot house; even a normally heated room is a little too hot for this plant. The deep dish method is excellent. Lower a saucer upside down in a deep dish containing water. When the bottom of the saucer just emerges from the water place the plant on this artificial island. It is then just above the water but not in it. Do not spray as water might collect in the leaf bases and cause rotting. Throughout the flowering period the soil in the pot must be kept relatively damp. After flowering the plant needs some months' rest. As it is not a completely resting period, it will need a little water from time to time. If repotting is required, this is best done in early spring, towards the beginning of the new growing period. Do not use the ordinary potting compost but a special mixture of osmunda fibre, peat moss and rotted beech leaf-mould to which some rotted cow manure should be added when practicable.

Passiflora caerulea (Passion Flower)

137   These attractive plants occur in many varieties. Passiflora caerulea is recommended for indoor cultivation and is becoming very popular nowadays. The flowers are exquisitely beautiful. The name was given to them by early missionaries in South America because the flowers bore a fancied representation of the Passion of Christ. It is a real climber and it will do well if you fix a bent wire in the pot along which the plant can be guided. The beautiful flowers only last for one day, but this does not matter as with a sturdy plant flowers will open every day of the summer. In the summer it is better to put the plant outside and it can be plunged in the garden complete with pot. Place it in a warm and sunny position as the buds will only open when the plant has plenty of sun. The plant can remain outside from mid-May to mid-October after which it should be taken back indoors. Put it in a very moderately heated room, or even an unheated room, as long as it is frost free. It then does not require much water and it is quite normal for all the leaves to drop. In the early spring all the bare branches can be drastically pruned and repotting should take place. Use the normal potting compost and do not forget the broken crock at the bottom of the pot.

It is easy to propagate from cuttings. This should be done in spring, with young shoots approximately 3 inches long, which will root easily in a jam jar filled with water. Later the plants can be potted separately in small pots filled with good potting compost. They may grow into sizeable plants and require repotting once or twice into a larger pot. The plant should be fed with manure regularly during the summer.

Pereskia godseffiana (Leaf cactus)

138   Often Phyllocactus is called leaf cactus, but the name really belongs to Pereskia godseffiana. It is a very colourful indoor plant which is not so popular as yet. The foliage is of a golden-brown colouring and you will really enjoy it. At first glance it does not look like a cactus at all; there are sharp spines on thin stems. These thin stems are often used as stock on which to graft Zygocactus, where they grow away more successfully than when grown in the normal way from a cutting. You may be able to order a Pereskia from a good florist.

The plant can be placed in full sunlight and does not need any protection in the summer, not even when placed on a window sill facing South. Full sunlight is necessary if the leaves turn to a fine bronze colour. If the plant is placed in too dark a place, the leaves will become green. The plant will flourish in a normally heated room.

A humid atmosphere is essential and frequent spraying with tepid water is most beneficial. The soil in the pot should be kept moist, but the watering should be reduced in wintertime. The plant can be propagated from cuttings using young shoots approximately 3 inches long, which will root quite easily when placed in a small pot with sandy soil. If older plants develop long straggly shoots, these may be pruned back during early spring. This is also the time for repotting. Use good potting compost.

Pelargonium grandiflorum (French Geranium)

139 Pelargonium grandiflorum is popular as a houseplant. It is known as French Geranium on the Continent. There are many varieties, some of which have such beautiful flowers that they recall those of orchids. The varieties with large pink flowers with red and dark spots are very popular. This type of geranium is more delicate and not quite so easy to grow as the better known varieties. It is not so successful as a garden plant, as the open flowers do not stand up the rain very well. As an indoor plant it still needs considerable care. Its position is too warm during the winter and early summer, it may be attacked by aphids. Nowadays there are many efficient sprays available to combat this pest. The plant cannot survive draught, so please do not open windows and doors at the same time. In the early spring flowering plants should be readily available which is the best time to obtain them. Place them on a sunny window sill, where the windows are opened frequently, as they require a lot of fresh air. The soil in the pot must be kept moist and a weekly dose of manure during the summer months is beneficial. During the winter, or preferably just before the winter, the plant should be cut back a little. The plant should be repotted in the spring, using good potting compost. Press the soil firmly in the pot. Propagation from cuttings is easily achieved and can best be done in early spring. Young shoots of approximately 3 inches may be put in a small pot with sandy soil to root. They will have to be potted on later into a larger pot.

Pelargonium zonale (Geranium)

140   These Pelargoniums are usually called geraniums. Theoretically this name is incorrect although it persists. The varieties with large flowers are very popular and appear in various colours. The bright red coloured variety is very attractive, but the orange and pink colours are also appealing. Geraniums can be grown both in the garden and indoors. The types with large flowers prefer a sunny position in the garden during the summer months, where they can be plunged complete with pot.

If the large flowered Geranium is kept indoors, it still needs a very sunny position. It will do very well on a window sill facing East and needs no protection. If grown facing South, it may become too hot for it, especially if the curtains are drawn behind it. Not only does the temperature rise too high, but the atmosphere becomes too dry and the flower buds shrivel up.

They are easily propagated from cuttings. This is best done in July-August, but can take place in the early spring. Young shoots of approximately 4 inches will root easily in a small pot filled with sandy soil. Later they need potting on into a bigger pot. The Geranium needs watering freely during the summer but this may be reduced in the winter, when feeding must also cease. Early spring is the time for vigorous cutting back and repotting into good potting compost.

Pelargonium zonale Black Vesuvius (Horseshoe Geranium or Zonal Geranium)

141   Miniature varieties of Geraniums are very popular nowadays, Black Vesuvius being one of the best known ones. This is a splendid flowering plant, with bright red flowers set against dark-brown foliage. It can be expected to flower almost throughout the year It needs, of course, a sunny position and it can stand much more sun than the large flowered varieties. Do not put the plant in too hot a position. A normally heated room is not suitable for this variety; it thrives much better in a very moderately heated one.

It is easily propagated from cuttings. This is best done in July, but can be done during the spring. Young shoots 2 to 3 inches long will root fairly quickly when placed in a small pot with sandy soil. Later they need a slightly larger pot. Do not forget the crock at the bottom of the pot as the drainage hole should not be blocked.

It is better not to transplant this variety to the garden in the summer, as they much prefer a sunny position on a window sill. Keep the soil in the pot moist and a weekly small dose of diluted liquid manure is greatly appreciated. There are also varieties nowadays with pink and white as well as dark red flowers. Remove the dead flowers regularly to encourage new flowers to appear.

Pellaea rotundifolia (Cliff Brake Fern)

142 This plant does not look like a fern at all. It is a very pleasant plant which you will enjoy for years. The roots are very near the surface and it does not need a deep pot. This is the reason why the florist often uses this fern when making up troughs of plants. If you only have a deep pot, you must fill one third of it with broken crocks.

As with other ferns, this variety also needs humid warmth as well as protection against direct sunlight. It will do well in a normally heated room, although it prefers a lower temperature. The plant should be kept moist; if it is placed in the living room the small leaves should be moistened daily with tepid water. There are very handy spraying devices available nowadays, which are specially designed for this purpose.

Propagation is simply done by dividing the plant. A suitable time is early spring, when large plants should be removed from their pots and divided into sections after which each section can be potted separately. They require a very nutritious soil mixture so use a good potting compost. If the plant develops dead leaves, the atmosphere is too dry and more spraying is required. You can use the deep-dish method of growth. A saucer is lowered upside down in a deep dish filled with water. When the bottom of the saucer is just above the water level, place the pot on this small island.

Pellionia pulchra

143   This small plant is a native of Cochin China. The green leaves are delicately veined and it is most successful as a house plant. It really is a creeper by nature but it can also be grown as a hanging plant. It requires warmth and should therefore be grown in a normally heated room in a very humid atmosphere. It should do well with the deep-dish method, where a saucer is lowered upside down in a deep dish filled with water. When the bottom of the saucer is just above the water level, the plant can be placed on this. The plant is then just above the water but not in it. Direct sunlight is detrimental to the plant and protection must be provided from mid-March to mid-October.

It is easy to propagate this plant from cuttings. This should be done in the spring or early summer. Young shoots approximately 3 inches long will root easily in a small pot with sandy soil. Pellionia requires a lot of nourishment and it is essential to administer a small dose of diluted manure weekly. Repotting may take place in the spring, using good potting compost mixed with a little peat-moss and if possible rotted cow manure as the plant thrives on rich, aerated soil. Do not forget the crock at the bottom of the pot. There are other varieties but these are not so suitable for cultivation in the house.

Peperomia caperata

144 Peperomia caperata is a very popular little plant nowadays. As it does not require much space, it is extremely suitable for a narrow window sill. The leaves are emerald green and look most attractive when the plant is in full flower.

This plant can easily be propagated by making leaf cuttings. Fully grown leaves are removed from the mother plant with a small piece of stem and then placed in a small pot filled with sandy soil until the leaves themselves rest on the surface. Place a plastic bag over the pot and roots will soon develop; when there are sufficient roots, the young plant will develop easily.

This plant thrives in a normally heated room but requires a humid atmosphere. Frequent spraying is necessary which should be done with tepid water. The soil in the pot should be kept moist. The florist has kept this plant away from bright sunlight and it should therefore be protected against direct sunshine.

Propagation by means of division is also possible, this is done in early spring. A fully grown plant is removed from its pot and divided into sections. Each section is planted separately. The plant needs a lot of nourishment and a weekly dose of diluted liquid manure is beneficial. Cultivation in deep pots is not very satisfactory, it is much better to use a shallow pot or bowl. If you only have a deep pot, fill one third of it with broken crocks.

Peperomia marmorata

145 There are many Peperomia species, which have their own special attraction. Peperomia marmorata is cultivated as an indoor plant and the florist often uses it when making up mixed plant bowls. They like a shallow bowl and when the other plants have died off you can remove it carefully and pot it separately. They do not like deep pots. If you only have medium sized pots, fill them for one third with broken crocks.

The typical yellow-white flower spikes are not impressive to look at but give a certain attraction to the plant. Its main glory is in its leaves which are richly coloured with finely drawn veins. When cultivating Peperomias do not forget that direct sunlight is detrimental to them and from March onwards they need protection. However, they do appreciate a light position. The plant does not need much room and a narrow window sill is ideal. It needs a lot of warmth and a normally heated room is an excellent place for it. It can be propagated from cuttings, which are best taken in early spring or summer. Leaf cuttings are very successful. The fully grown leaves are removed from the mother plant complete with stem. They are placed right up to the leaf itself in a small pot filled with sandy soil. Place a plastic bag over the pot. After a while you will notice a young plant developing from the leaf.

Pernettya mucronata

146 You really should not consider this Pernettya as a normal house plant, since it is an evergreen small shrub which grows very well in the open in your garden. It can be kept indoors as a temporary visitor and should not be placed in a normally heated room as the temperature there will be much too high. Excellent results may be achieved when it is cultivated in a slightly warm room, or even an unheated place, so long as it is frost-free. There are a number of varieties, either with red or white berries. You will enjoy it specially if you have a garden, as the shrub can be planted outside afterwards.

The root system should be kept moist and a weekly dose of diluted liquid manure does no harm at all. It should only be watered with lukewarm water in a cold room and not with cold water. When the beautiful berries are over, the plant can be plunged in the garden. It requires full sunlight and it should be placed in a sheltered and sunny position. Not every type of soil is suitable as it requires a peaty soil. You can, of course, fill the area around the plant with a mixture of peat-mould, rotted manure and sharp sand. Protection should be given it against too severe frost; spruce branches will do this very well. Pernettyas may be propagated from cuttings, but you must then use a potting compost which is specially mixed for such plants.

Philodendron panduriforme

147 A number of Philodendrons are now grown and make very decorative house plants. Most of them require quite a lot of space as they grow very wide. You will enjoy them in a garden room.

Philodendron should not be grown at a low temperature as it needs lots of warmth and a humid atmosphere. Frequent spraying is essential, and this should be done with tepid water and never with cold water straight from the tap. The soil in the pot should be kept moist and for this purpose tepid water must also be used.

Philodendron cannot stand direct sunlight and it needs protection from mid-April to mid-October. As the plant is usually supplied in a pot which is too small, it will not grow to its normal size and potting on is necessary. Use a good potting compost mixed with a little peat-mould and chopped peat-moss as the plant likes a rich, well-aerated soil mixture. Do not forget the crocks at the bottom of the pot. If the plant is happy, if will form aerial roots which should not be cut off. If the plant grows too wide, you can control it by cutting it back and taking the top out. This has been done in the illustration. The top is planted complete with aerial roots in a pot with aerated soil. The old plant will then develop new shoots. Older plants can be maintained by a small weekly dose of diluted liquid manure.

Philodendron wendlandii

148 There are many Philodendron varieties, some of which require more warmth than others. This variety can stand a considerable amount of warmth and should be kept in a normally heated room. It does not look like a Philodendron from its leaves but it is a beautiful plant which you will be able to enjoy for a long time, as long as it is kept warm and moist. The fairly wide leaves need frequent spraying. This should be done daily and tepid water should be used. The soil in the pot must be kept moist by watering with luke-warm water. The plant requires plenty of feeding and a small dose of diluted manure weekly is essential. Dissolve one teaspoon of liquid manure in two pints of water, this is sufficient for approximately 20 plants. If repotting is necessary, this should be done in early spring. Use a good potting compost but add a little additional peat-mould and rotted cow manure as the plant appreciates rich, well-aerated soil. Direct sunlight is detrimental. Protection from early spring onwards is essential and should be continued to mid-September.

It is possible to propagate it from cuttings, for which purpose the stems should be used. This is not easily done in a room, but a miniature greenhouse is excellent for the purpose. You could try it in a room, but the cuttings require bottom heat. You may be successful in making the stems root in moist moss.

Phyllocactus ackermannii (Epiphyllum)

149 This leaf cactus is a native of Central America and Mexico and is cultivated very successfully as a house plant. The bright red flowers are most attractive and produced freely. This plant is also known by the name Epiphyllum. During the winter the plant needs a rather cool environment and a room which is just frost-free is sufficient. A moderately heated room is still acceptable but the plant will not survive in a normally heated room. It needs a complete rest during the winter months from November to mid-February, which is the reason for the cool place. It has to form flower buds at these lower temperatures and it is necessary to reduce the watering and cease the manuring altogether. Spraying is helpful but this should only be done with tepid water. It is sufficient to water the plant once every three weeks. It needs a sunny position, even though the room is cool. Do not turn the plant during the resting period, otherwise the flower buds will be lost.

When the leaves are full of flower buds the plant can be removed to the living room, and the flowers will soon open and normal watering should take place. After flowering it should continue to grow rapidly. It can be repotted after flowering, if necessary. Do not use cactus soil for this purpose but normal potting compost. Leaves which have grown too lanky can be cut back and you can use them as cuttings. During the summer protection against direct sunlight is essential and the plant can be removed complete with its pot into the garden, where it can be plunged in light shade. There are also varieties with large white or pink flowers.

Pilea cadierei

150   This decorative house plant which comes from Indo-China has become very popular lately because of its beautiful silver-coloured leaves. The plant does not grow very tall, nor very wide, so it fits easily into a small space. It requires a good deal of warmth and can easily be grown in a normally heated room, even though it requires a very humid atmosphere. The colourful leaf should be sprayed daily with tepid water. The plant needs to be watered freely and if planted in a small pot it will dry out sooner than expected. Water regularly with tepid water. During the winter months in particular a humid atmosphere is essential. The deep-dish method is very useful. A saucer is lowered upside down in a deep dish containing water. When the bottom of the saucer is just above the water level, the plant can be placed on this little island. The plant needs protection against direct sunlight during the summer. The leaves tend to turn black and drop during the winter, but you can prune back drastically during early spring. There is no specific height to prune back to, so choose the height you like best. The plant should also be repotted then, using good potting compost. After six weeks you may start to give it a small dose of diluted liquid manure. The young shoots removed after pruning may be used as cuttings. Put them in a jam jar filled with water, where they will root quickly. When they have sufficient roots, the plants can be potted separately into small pots filled with good potting compost. You may also put 3 to 5 small plants in a medium sized pot, when the plant will become thick and bushy.

Pilea spruceana

151   This plant is much less frequently grown than Pilea cadierei. There is no real reason for this, as it is a charming little plant with bronzy leaves which have strange indentations of the surface. The plant forms many shoots which all grow upright. These shoots make propagation a simple job. Young shoots approximately 3 inches long will root easily when placed in a small pot with sandy soil.

Pilea spruceana needs plenty of warmth and should be cultivated in a normally heated room; it also needs a lot of moisture and therefore frequent spraying with tepid water, which is essential to create a humid atmosphere. Keep the soil in the pot damp by watering with tepid water. If the plant is restricted to too small a pot, it will never develop properly. It also can be grown in a shallow bowl. You should fill this with a good potting compost mixed with some peat as an aerated soil is necessary. Do not forget to place some crocks at the bottom of the bowl. The plant needs protection from direct sunlight from mid-April onwards but towards mid-October the full sun is beneficial. Some leaves may drop during the winter, but they will be replaced in early spring. If the plant becomes stripped of leaves at the base, you can use the tops for cuttings. Flowering may possibly occur but the flowers are insignificant.

Platycerium bifurcatum (Stag's Horn fern)

152   Platycerium is much better known by its common name: Stag's Horn fern. There are many species but bifurcatum is the most popular house plant, and it can be cultivated in many ways. The plant may be grown on a piece of light-weight bark or a beech log. The florist will have provided this with a wad of moist moss and if this can be mixed with some rotted cow manure, the plant will thrive. Watering can be a bit of a problem if the plant is hanging on the wall. Place it twice a week in a bowl filled with lukewarm water to which some liquid manure has been added. It may remain there for a quarter of an hour and then be allowed to drip dry. As this method is rather awkward, the plant can be grown successfully in pots nowadays. Watering can then take place in the normal way. They do not require much water and an application every other day is sufficient. The plant should be grown at normal room temperature.

In tropical forests the Stag's Horn ferns grow high up in trees, and for this reason the plant cannot stand much sunlight, so from mid-March onwards protection is required. The florist grows the plant from spores, but large indoor plants may be propagated by splitting them. When repotting is necessary, use a mixture of chopped peat-moss, osmunda fibre and rotted beech leaf-mould to which, if possible, some rotted cow-manure has been added. Do not forget a layer of crocks in the bottom of the pot.

Plumbago capensis (Cape Leadwort)

153 Plumbago capensis is a beautiful climber which is nowadays very popular for sunny rooms. The clusters of white or lilac flowers resemble Phlox. This plant can either be cultivated in a normally heated or in a moderately heated room. It needs a humid atmosphere and regular spraying with tepid water is therefore essential. It may flower right through the summer, but towards the winter many leaves will drop. This is quite normal and is no reason for anxiety. As the plant is entering its resting period, watering should be reduced and manuring must stop altogether. In the early spring you should cut it back, as this vigorous climber can produce such extensive shoots that it becomes over-powering. Repotting can take place at the same time as the pruning. Use the normal potting compost and do not forget the crocks on top of the drainage hole in the bottom of the pot.

Propagation by taking cuttings is an easy job. Take some young shoots approximately 3 inches long and place them in a jar filled with water. When there are sufficient roots you can plant each cutting into an individual medium sized pot filled with good potting compost. The older plants need a weekly dose of diluted liquid manure. Plumbago is not difficult to obtain in this country, and is becoming popular. The white flowered variety is extremely rare but as the lilac flower is much more attractive this does not really matter.

Polypodium crispum glaucum (Polypody or Blue Fern)

154　Many ferns originate in forests and mostly tropical or sub-tropical forests at that. They often grow underneath or on the massive trees and this should not be forgotten when cultivating them indoors. This is one of the most beautiful Polypodium varieties with curly, blue tinted leaves. It is a very decorative plant which may require a larger space as time goes on, and it should therefore be placed in a position in which the leaves are not constantly touched.

The plant must be kept in a normally heated room. Daily spraying with lukewarm water is necessary. Never use cold water straight from the tap. Underneath the leaves spores develop in small brown areas which are easily mistaken for aphids. Aphids can be removed with a damp brush and some soapy water; if this does not work there are many very effective sprays available in the shops.

The soil in the pot should be kept damp and repotting is necessary in the spring. Use normal potting compost but mix it with a little peat-mould and, if possible, rotted cow manure, the plant thrives on well-aerated, rich nutritious soil. Protection against direct sunlight is essential.

Polystichum falcatum (Cyrtomium falcatum)

155 Polystichum falcatum is often called Cyrtomium falcatum. This is a very hardy fern which will thrive in a moderately heated room. Generally speaking, ferns are not so suitable for cultivation as indoor plants. One often forgets that these plants really belong to the forest and require a very moist atmosphere and definitely no direct sunlight. This variety is a native of Japan and requires less warmth than other ferns. For this reason it will thrive in an unheated bedroom, so long as the room is frost-free. The plants may also be placed in an unheated hall.

The plant grows vigorously and needs weekly feeding. You can use a well-known liquid manure for house plants. However, this is on its own not sufficient and in the spring the plants will have to be repotted. Use a good quality potting compost mixed with some rotted leaf-mould, as the plant likes an aerated soil mixture. Do not forget to place some crocks over the drainage hole in the bottom of the pot, this hole must not be blocked. The underside of leaves of older plants may be covered in brown areas of spores and it is much better to remove these, as if they blow away they may cause trouble.

Propagation by dividing the plant is easy and should be done in early spring. Remove the large plant carefully from its pot and divide it into sections. Each section should have roots and leaves and can be planted separately in an individual pot.

Primula obconica

156   This is a well known and much liked Primula species, which will give pleasure for months and can be kept for the next season. But there are people who cannot stand this plant as it may cause a skin irritation.

The plant is easy to grow and occurs in many colours. The red and white varieties are very popular in the Christmas season, but the pink, lilac and blue colours are also in great demand. The florist cultivates this plant away from direct sunlight and once in your home it will need the same protection. During the winter sunlight is not so harmful but the plant always needs light. A normally heated room is really a little too hot, the plant preferring a moderately heated one. Even though the florist has supplied the plant in good potting compost, you will have to supplement this with a weekly dose of diluted liquid manure if you want the plant to go on flowering. Free watering is necessary and you should use tepid water for this. Do not spray flowering plants. When flowering has ceased, the plant may be repotted. Use a good potting compost but make sure there is no oakleaf-mould in it, as the plant cannot endure this. During the summer the plant can be plunged in the garden, in a slightly shady position. In mid-October it has to be taken indoors. Primula malacoides is another species which is quite pleasing, but which cannot be kept throughout the winter. It is propagated by means of seed. Protect this plant also from strong sunlight and water a flowering plant several times daily.

Primula sinensis (Chinese Primula)

157   Some people think this plant old-fashioned, but as a profusely flowering house plant it is very pleasing. Naturally it is extremely tempting to buy a plant which is in full flower, however, it is much better to resist this temptation and buy a plant with only a few open flowers and many buds since you will enjoy it for much longer. There are many coloured varieties of this species, the salmon-coloured one particularly is in great demand. The florist grows this plant from seed. If you have a miniature greenhouse you will be able to do this yourself. Primula seeds have to germinate in the dark. When the seedlings show, they should be pricked out carefully; at a later stage they can all be potted into small individual pots, filled with good potting compost. If you sow in June, you will have flowering plants well before the winter. You can also sow in the autumn, when you will have your flowering plants in the spring. Do not keep the plant at a temperature which is too high, a normally heated room is too warm for it; it thrives in moderate heat. The florist will have supplied this plant in a good potting compost, but if you wish it to go on flowering a little encouragement can be given by a weekly dose of diluted liquid manure. It needs lots of water, but do not spray flowering plants. To prevent the colour of the leaves turning pale, you must protect the plant against direct sunlight. The plant can be overwintered, but it should then be repotted after flowering in good potting compost. Do not forget the crocks in the bottom of the pot. The soil should be pressed firmly around the plants in the pots.

Pteris cretica

158   Pteris cretica is a very hardy fern which you can keep for years. The florist often uses this fern in combination with other plants in a plant bowl, troughs or baskets. After a while you may want to remove the fern and grow it on its own. Nearly all ferns originate in tropical and sub-tropical forests. This is the reason why they should never be placed in direct sunlight in the house but do require a light place, especially during the winter. They also need a moist atmosphere, which makes daily spraying essential. The soil in the pot has to be kept damp as ferns need a lot of water, which must be tepid. The plants are usually supplied in pots which are too small and they then need to be repotted. Use good quality potting compost mixed with a little peat-mould, as ferns thrive on an aerated, rich soil mixture. With all this rich soil, the plant still requires additional nourishment and a little diluted liquid manure should be administered once a week from early spring to late autumn. If repotting is necessary, this is best done during early spring or summer. Use potting compost and do not forget the crocks in the bottom of the pot. Propagation can be done by splitting the plant, this can be combined with the repotting. Remove large plants from their pots and divide them into sections.

Pteris tremula

159   This fern is a native of Australia and New Zealand and is a great favourite as an indoor plant. The large leaves are very feathery and resemble those of carrots. The plant may become large and reach a height of over 2 feet, so you must allow it plenty of space to develop. Small plants look very attractive; they grow quickly and soon have to be repotted into a larger pot.

Ferns grown as indoor plants must be shaded from the sun, as they were in their original surroundings in the forests. Even when placed on a window-sill facing East, protection is needed from mid-April onwards, right up to October. During the winter the sun cannot do much harm. The temperature in a normally heated room is too warm and the plant must be removed to a very moderately heated room to be successful. Watering must be done with tepid water and the soil in the pot must be kept damp. Frequent watering during the summer months is essential. The root formation dries out sooner than you expect. You may lose some leaves during the winter, but this is not a serious problem, as they will quickly be replaced during the spring. Repotting must be done immediately prior to this. Use normal potting compost mixed with a little peat-mould, and rotted cow manure if you have it, as the plant requires a nutritious but well-aerated soil. It needs plenty of food in addition to that in the soil, for this reason you should supply it once a week with a small dose of diluted liquid manure.

Punica granatum (Pomegranate)

160 Punica granatum is the pomegranate. In the East it can grow very tall. You may have seen the plant in full flower by the Mediterranean, where it is an attractive sight. The bright red flowers look extremely decorative against the pale green foliage. As a house plant this species is very successful. During the summer months you can plunge the plant, complete with pot, in the garden, in a sunny position. Water freely during the summer but this must be drastically reduced during the winter months. The resting period begins during the autumn when watering and manuring can cease. The plant will shed all its leaves, but this is natural. The plant needs a complete rest and it is best to place it in an unheated, frost-free room. It does not need much sun. In the early spring the plant must be removed from its pot, the stale and dry earth shaken away from its roots and repotted into a good potting compost. Very soon you will discover new growth and you may start weekly manuring. The plant may be propagated from cuttings, which should be taken in the early spring. Young shoots approximately 3 inches long will root fairly easily. If you keep the plant indoors during the summer, it needs a little shading during the hottest part of the day.

Pyrrheimia loddigesii (Tradescantia fuscata)

161   There are several plants of this family which are now available for indoor cultivation. This plant thrives in the house but should be kept in a moderately heated room. Most growers call this plant Tradescantia fuscata. Its growth is not at all like that of the usual Tradescantia. The leaves are thickly covered with brown-red hairs and may have white to silver-grey veins and flowers which are blue or red. It is an extremely decorative plant which is the reason for its popularity. Propagation by division is best done in the early spring. Remove the plant from the pot and divide it into sections. You may be able to do this by hand, otherwise use a knife. Each section with roots and leaves can be potted again in normal potting compost. Do not press the soil down too much as the plant prefers aerated soil.

The plant must be shaded from bright sunlight. You must start to do this in mid-April and continue until mid-September, but from then onwards full sun will be appreciated. It is beneficial to the plant to receive a weekly dose of diluted liquid manure, especially during the early spring and summer. Like most Tradescantias it can stand a lot of water and the soil in the pot should be kept damp. Spraying of the hairy leaves is not good.

Rhipsalidopsis gaertneri (Schlumbergera gaertneri)

162 At first glance this cactus resembles the Zygocactus or Christmas cactus but the plant flowers in the spring. Specialists still do not agree about its Latin name and this plant is also sometimes called Epiphyllopsis gaertneri. It grows high up in trees in the forks of branches, which is the reason why normal cactus soil mixture is not suitable for its growth. Use ordinary potting compost mixed with a little peat-mould. The best method of propagating is to take cuttings. The segments of the stem can easily be removed after flowering and they root well in a small pot with sandy soil. Afterwards repot the small plants. Often the plant is grafted, and this can be done onto the lower stem of Pereskia or the real leaf cactus.

The plant should be kept growing right through the autumn and winter. Allow it to rest after mid-February by reducing the watering and cease to add liquid manure. As soon as the red flower buds appear, the watering can be increased, but spraying is not very beneficial then. Once the flower buds have appeared, the plant should not be turned any more; its angle towards the sun should remain the same, and some shading is necessary against too strong sunlight. You may plunge the plant, complete with pot, in a shady spot in the garden during the summer months. Towards mid-October the plant must come indoors again into a moderately heated room. If repotting is needed, this is best done immediately after flowering.

Rhododendron obtusum (Azalea obtusa - Japanese azalea)

163   Rhododendron obtusum is usually called the Japanese azalea. The beautiful shape of this very free flowering plant makes it attractive for cultivation as a house plant. There are many colours, of which the pinks, lilacs and reds are particularly attractive. They generally flower from March to May, which is the right time to buy a plant. It needs protection from direct sunlight and is best in a cool room. The fibrous soil should be kept moist. Do not spray during flowering, but daily spraying of the plant after flowering is beneficial. The plant can be planted in the open ground of the garden after mid-May; put a mixture of garden soil, rotted cow manure and peat-mould in the hole before putting the plant in it. Daily watering during the summer months is still a necessity outdoors and if it does not rain, spraying should be kept up. You can lift the plant in mid-October with enough root-soil to plant it firmly in a wide pot. At first the plant must be kept in an un-heated frost-free room. Keep the soil in the pot moist and administer the weekly dose of diluted liquid manure, also continue to spray. When the temperature drops the plant can be removed to a slightly warm room. If, however, the temperature is too high in the room, the leaves will turn yellow and drop. Green shoots develop next to the flower buds and these must be removed before flowering. After flowering, they should be left as they produce the flower buds of the next season.

Rhododendron simsii (Azalea simsii, Indoor Azalea)

164   This well-known indoor azalea is really a Rhododendron but no housewife will call it by that name.

Azaleas occur in many varieties and colours. There are early and late flowering varieties and ones with single or double flowers. You will enjoy the Azalea as it can be kept for a long time and it overwinters well. After flowering the plant should be placed in a cool position and in mid-May it can go into the garden in the open soil. Make a fair-sized hole and fill it with a mixture of decomposed leaf-mould, peat-moss and rotted cow manure. Water and spray the plant regularly. In mid-October the plant should be lifted with all the adhering soil and placed in a wide pot. Place the pot first in a sunny spot in a cool but frost-free room. Often Azaleas fail because people are in too much of a hurry; the flower buds must be really firm before the plant can be placed in a normally heated room. Early flowering varieties can stand a higher temperature in December, the later flowering ones only in the spring. Next to the flower buds small green shoots develop, they divert all the nutriment which is meant for the flower buds, which then dry up and die. This is the reason why these shoots should be removed before flowering. After flowering they can be left as they form the buds for the flowers of next year. Frequent spraying with tepid water is essential in developing the flower buds. As long as the plant is not in full flower, a weekly dose of diluted liquid manure is beneficial.

Rhoeo spathacea

165   This multi-coloured, decorative plant comes from Mexico and Florida and is related to Tradescantia. The beautifully coloured leaves are dark red underneath with green and yellow stripes above and are more attractive than the lilac-white flowers. It is a vigorous plant which thrives both in a normally heated room and in a moderately heated one. The plant stands plenty of water and the soil in the pot should be kept damp. Always use tepid water as the plant just cannot stand cold tap-water. The plant needs a lot of nourishment which makes a weekly dose of diluted liquid manure very beneficial.

Propagation is easily carried out by using young shoots as cuttings. Older plants form young plants at the base. When these are about 4 inches high, they can be removed carefully from the mother plant and planted in a small pot with sandy soil. They will root very well and grow quickly so that you will soon have to provide them with a larger pot. Use the normal potting compost mixed with a little additional rotted cow manure and peat-mould. Old plants can easily deteriorate and if this occurs you must renew your plant by rooting cuttings. This is best done in the spring or during the summer months.

Rhoicissus rhombifolia (Grape ivy)

166   Nowadays there is a great interest in this kind of climbing plant. Rhoicissus resembles Cissus antarctica in that it is a rapid grower which will cover a large space of wall surface in a short time. The plant is usually supplied in a pot which is too small and you would be well advised to repot it straight away as once the plant is established against your wall it is not a very easy job to do. If you do not wish the plant to grow directly on to the wall, you can erect a trellis or net which may enhance the decorative aspect of your room. The plant will easily trail along and through it.

When repotting use good potting compost. Press the plant firmly into the pot, otherwise the soil will dry out readily. It needs plenty of water, so keep the soil in the pot damp with tepid water. The plant thrives both in normally heated livingrooms as well as in moderately heated ones. Everybody has some corners which are dull and uninteresting and where many plants will not grow. Such a corner is ideal for Rhoicissus so long as some light is provided during the daytime, such as that of a small lamp of 20 watts.

The plant likes a humid atmosphere and regular spraying with tepid water is essential. It cannot stand strong sunlight. If the shoots become too overpowering, they can be cut back and used as cuttings to propagate the plant.

Rochea coccinea

167   Rochea is a succulent with scarlet flowers which look very attractive during the summer months. Complaints that the plant cannot be made to flower are usually due to incorrect treatment. The plant does not grow during the winter and during this time it is sufficient to water it just enough for the plant to remain green and alive. It should not be placed in a warm place; a slightly warm room is good enough, although it does even better in an unheated but frost-free room. Watering in this cool environment must be done with tepid water and manuring should cease altogether, as it stimulates new growth.

You can increase the amount of water given in the spring and from April onwards water freely and also start weekly manuring. Even though the plant can tolerate the sun, it needs some shading from mid-April onwards, otherwise black spots will develop on the leaves. Shading becomes essential when the plant is in flower, otherwise the flowers will fade to a pale pink, which is less attractive. After flowering, cut back heavily and repot in good potting compost. The plant can be propagated by making cuttings of the young shoots. These can be placed in a small pot with sandy soil, where they root easily. During the following season these young plants have to be repotted to a larger size pot.

Ruellia devosiana (Christmas Pride)

168   There are many varieties of this family, some of which originate in tropical America. Some species are cultivated as indoor plants. Ruellia devosiana has olive green leaves with a delicate network of veins, while the underside of the leaf is reddish in colour. This is the main attraction of this small plant. The flowers are white tinted with rose on short stalks and they have lilac veins. They appear during late autumn and winter. It needs a normally heated room and a humid atmosphere, so spraying is essential and tepid water should be used, as the cold water straight from the tap will harm the plant.

Propagation of the Ruellia is by means of cuttings. These can be taken in early spring; young shoots approximately 3 inches long will root quite easily in a small pot with sandy soil. Old, overwintered plants must be cut back a little in the early spring, when they also need to be repotted. Use the normal potting compost and do not forget the crocks in the bottom of the pot.

The plant cannot stand direct sunlight and needs shading from mid-March to mid-October. Plants which have not been repotted must be manured once a week with a small dose of diluted liquid manure.

Saintpaulia ionantha (African violet)

169   This is a pleasing little plant, which with the right treatment will flower almost throughout the year. There may be some weeks during the winter when there are no flowers but early spring there will be an abundance of them. There used to be only the blue varieties, but now white and red and pink flowered varieties are to be seen and all are equally attractive. The African violet requires a humid atmosphere and a normally heated room. It can best be grown with the so-called deep-dish method. Lower a saucer upside down into a deep dish containing water until the bottom of the saucer just emerges above the water level. Place the plant on this small island, it is now above the water but not in it and the humidity around the plant is considerably increased. Use tepid water for spraying. Keep the soil in the pot damp, but for watering never use cold water straight from the tap.

Draught is detrimental to African violets. Coloured markings and spots will develop on the leaves which will increase in size. It also needs protection against too strong sunlight and even in March the sun is already harmful. The plant does, however, require a light position. Leaf cuttings are a good method of propagation. An adult leaf is removed complete with a small stem section and put into a small pot containing sandy soil, in such a way that the stem is buried and the leaf lies flat on the soil. Cover the pot with a plastic bag. After some months a young plant will appear.

Sanchezia nobilis

170 This plant comes from South America and is very decorative in the house. Its main attraction are its leaves, which are bright and glossy with strongly marked veins. Late in the autumn flowers appear which are yellow with bright red bracts. This plant needs quite a lot of warmth and requires a very humid atmosphere, so the large leaves must be sprayed daily with tepid water. The plant should be watered freely and the soil in the pot must be kept moist. Never use cold water straight from the tap, as this will harm the plant; the water must be tepid. The plant cannot stand strong sunlight and shade has to be provided after mid-April, otherwise the leaves will 'burn' and go limp. However, they do need a light position and they can tolerate the sun after mid-October. As the plant grows vigorously, it must be manured regularly. Use a well-known liquid manure, which should be diluted, one teaspoon to 2 pints of water, giving a sufficient quantity for about 20 plants. Early spring is the best time to propagate the plant from cuttings. Young shoots approximately 3 inches long will root easily when placed in a jam jar filled with water. When sufficient roots have developed, each plant can be put separately in a small pot filled with potting compost and later a larger pot is required. Do not forget the pieces of crock in the bottom of the pot. Normal repotting of adult plants should take place in the early spring, when straggly plants can be heavily pruned.

Sansevieria hahnii (Bowstring Hemp, Angola Hemp)

171 This low growing species does not require much room, but it grows well and is propagated easily. Sansevieria hahnii should not be placed in the direct sun. It can be left on a window sill facing East, but even there the green will fade eventually and it really needs protection after 10 o'clock in the morning. It will do well in a normally heated room and can also thrive in a slightly warm room but then one should water it less frequently. The plant cannot stand cold tap water, it must be at least tepid and you should remove surplus water from the saucer after a quarter of an hour. For the same reason you must not leave water in the bottom of a decorative cover-pot. The florist often places this plant together with other plants in a bowl or basket. After a while you can remove the Sansevieria and cultivate it separately.

Many shoots form at the base of the mother plant. When these are about 3 inches, they can be removed easily and grown separately in pots. Use good potting compost, mixed with a little sharp sand. Do not forget the crocks in the bottom of the pot.

The variegated leaved variety which is becoming popular needs a little more warmth.

Sansevieria trifasciata (Mother-in-law's tongue)

172   This is a decorative plant which is generally well-known, and can be kept for years. Propagation of the Sansevieria can be done relatively simply. Cut adult leaves in sections of 4 inches, place these in a small pot with sandy soil and eventually roots will form. Later the new leaves will appear and you may be disappointed since they are plain green without the decorative yellow edge of the original plant. If you want to preserve this appearance, you must propagate it in a different way and it is necessary to divide the plant. Adult plants may be removed from their pots and split into sections, each of which should have some leaves and roots. Planted separately, these plants will keep their original colouring.

Keep the Sansevieria in a normally heated room. Many die because they are kept too cold during the winter or are overwatered. It is sufficient during the winter to water them once every fortnight; this should be increased to once daily during the summer. Sansevierias do flower. They need protection against direct sunlight, otherwise the colour of the leaves fades; and they should have a weekly dose of diluted liquid manure.

Saxifraga cotyledon

173   Saxifraga cotyledon is a perennial plant which can be grown indoors or in the garden, although it is very popular nowadays as a house plant. The small rosettes of leaves are pleasant but in May-June the attractive flowering stems develop, sometimes only one, but very often there are several. Usually these stems are very weak and you have to support them with thin wire in order to keep them upright. The flower stems droop particularly when the position of the plant is too hot or too sunny. The stems will be sturdier with more shading from sunlight and more fresh air. These requirements reflect the origin of the plant in the northern regions. After flowering the stems can be removed and the main attraction of the plant is then gone. This does not really matter, because by that time many new rosettes have formed which you should allow to grow. Afterwards these rosettes can be potted separately in small pots with good potting compost mixed with a little heavy loam. These young plants which you have grown from the small rosettes can best be plunged in the garden, complete with pot, in a slightly shady place. Towards the end of October the plants should come indoors again to a sunny, unheated but frost-free room. They should be shaded against sunlight from mid-April onwards. It will be two or three years before the young plants flower.

Saxifraga stolonifera var. tricolor (Mother of thousands, Pedlar's basket)

174   This little plant was popular even in our grandmother's time, and now it forms a welcome gift to any lady. The ordinary green leaved species is quite hardy and can be cultivated in a slightly warm room. Young plants develop on very thin stems and can be removed complete with roots and grown separately. There is also a variegated form, Tricolor (shown here) which requires a little more warmth and consequently must be grown in the living room. The florist usually supplies this plant in a pot which is too small and it must therefore be repotted fairly quickly. Use a good potting compost mixed with a little peat-mould and sharp sand. Do not press the soil too firmly into the pot.

The plant likes a humid atmosphere, so frequent spraying is essential but use tepid water. The soil in the pot must be kept damp. The plant needs shading from the sun from mid-April to mid-October, otherwise the leaves will droop. The variegated form does not produce as many young plants on thin stems as the green one, however as the plant develops some will be produced. The plant should have a weekly dose of diluted liquid manure. It does not like deep pots and thrives best in a bowl or shallow flower pot.

Schefflera

175 This decorative plant is a native of Australia and has only recently been grown as an indoor plant. The plant resembles Hedera slightly but it is more elegant in shape. It is quite easy to grow, although the plant really prefers a slightly warm room it will grow at normal room temperatures. It will tolerate a fair amount of sun but needs some protection during the hottest part of the day. Keep the soil in the pot damp by watering daily. Frequent spraying is essential, especially when the plant is placed in a normally heated room, and the elegant leaves should be moistened daily with some tepid water.

This plant can be increased easily from seeds. These are not very easy to obtain, but they can be ordered. Sow at once in a pot filled with potting compost, in a warm room. Cover the pot with a sheet of glass and some paper. When germination has taken place, remove both glass and paper. Later on the seedlings can be potted in small pots and a little later on this size of pot will become too small and a larger size is needed. Use good potting compost. The plant will grow to a fairly large size, so a wide pot is essential. It needs plenty of nourishment and therefore requires a weekly dose of diluted liquid manure.

Scindapsus aureus

176 A tall climber from the Solomon Islands which has much-branched stems and leaves mottled with gold. It quite obviously belongs to the Aroid group. Cultivation in a normally heated room is essential but it needs also a very humid atmosphere. The leaves should be sprayed daily with tepid water, never use cold water straight from the tap. The plant will not tolerate strong sunlight and needs shading a little from mid-April. However, its position should be light, otherwise the mottled leaves will turn green all over and lose their attraction.

It is a very sturdy climber and it is best used as such. If you place a bent wire in the pot, the long shoots can be trained around it. If the long shoots become too profuse, they may be drastically pruned. This is best done during early spring or early summer. The spare shoots can be used as cuttings by placing them in a jar filled with water. They will root easily and afterwards they can be planted in small pots filled with potting compost mixed with some peat-mould. Older plants can be kept healthy by giving them a weekly dose of diluted liquid manure.

Sometimes this plant is seen in a plant-bowl together with other plants. If you wish to grow it on its own, it can be removed carefully together with the earth which hangs to its roots, and potted separately.

Sedum sieboldii

177   Like most succulents, this is a very easy plant to grow. The leaves are blue-grey in colour or in the variety medio variegatum pink with white to yellow blotches in the middle. The blue variety is most popular. They do not require much warmth and in the winter they can be kept in a sunny position in an unheated, but frost-free room. This little plant may flower in the depth of winter when it produces pink on red starlet flowers which remain fresh for a long time.

When it has finished flowering, the dead flowers should be cut off in early spring and the plant can be repotted. Use the normal potting compost or the special cactus soil mixture. If necessary the plant may be divided when you repot and the various pieces grown separately.

The plant is easily propagated from cuttings. Young shoots of approximately 3 inches long will root without difficulty when placed in a small pot of sandy soil. Later they will need potting on into a larger pot. You may also cut up the stem into pieces 1 to 2 inches long, and if they are placed, complete with some leaves, in a pot containing sandy soil, they too will form roots. As this plant does not need much warmth, you may plunge it in the garden in its pot from mid-April onwards. Give it a sunny position. You should not have much trouble in obtaining this plant.

The variety with the gold coloured leaves is even hardier. It can tolerate a lower temperature and may be kept in the garden during a mild winter.

Selaginella (Tropical moss)

178   There are numerous species of Selaginella, some of which are grown with great success as house plants. At first glance the delicate foliage resembles that of an ordinary indoor fern, but they are tropical plants resembling moss. Since mosses usually require a very humid atmosphere and considerable warmth, this plant must be grown in a warm room. Frequent spraying is essential; use tepid water as cold water from the tap does endless harm. The soil in the pot should also be kept moist with lukewarm water.

Nearly always the florist has grown this plant in a pot which is far too small for it and you will have to repot it almost immediately after you receive it. Place a good layer of crocks in the bottom of the pot and fill up with good potting compost mixed with some peat-mould. Since these plants prefer a well-aerated soil, the soil must not be pressed down too firmly.

It can stand only a little direct sun and protection is needed from mid-March to mid-October. The plant can be propagated from cuttings made from the young shoots. These should not be too long, 2 inches is ample. The delightful golden effect of this little moss like plant makes it very popular in plant bowls or baskets when it will show the other plants off to advantage. There are also varieties which creep along the surface of the soil.

Senecio (Cineraria)

179 The Cineraria should really be called Senecio, but only botanists know it by that name. The layman calls the plant Cineraria or on the continent Ash-plant, which refers to the ash-coloured under surface of the leaves. Nowadays they are cultivated in numerous colours, of which both the single forms and the double ones are extremely attractive. There are varieties with large flowers and others with small ones. It is, of course, very tempting to buy a plant when it is fully in flower, yet it is much better to resist the temptation and buy a plant with many buds and only a few open flowers. The florist will have given the plant a good potting compost, but if you wish to prolong its flowering, you will have to administer a weekly dose of diluted lquid manure. Cinerarias require a light position but do not place them in bright sunlight as the leaves will droop at once and the flowers lose colour. The soil in the pot should be kept moist and the plant needs a lot of water.

A normally heated room is hotter than the plant can endure and it will thrive better in an unheated but frost-free room. Do not spray. If they are in a draughty position or the temperature is too high, they may become covered with aphids. Should this occur, you must spray them with a repellent which is readily available in any seed shop.

Setcreasea purpurea (Purple Heart)

180   This plant is very well-known, although people generally think it is a Tradescantia. The stems are rather weak and hairy, the leaves are rather long, purple coloured and hairy as well. The plant is easy to grow and it is propagated from cuttings. This is best done in the spring, but can also be performed in summer or autumn. The plant has an untidy growth, and if the stems have become straggly they can easily be cut back and used as cuttings in the autumn, since young plants overwinter better than old ones. Shoots of approximately 3 to 4 inches can be used. Put about seven cuttings to one normal sized pot, one in the centre and the remaining six around the sides of the pot; in this way you will soon have a nice bushy plant. Use good potting compost and, to encourage branching, pinch off the tops of the stems.

Not much warmth is required and a moderately heated room is sufficient. It can stand a fair amount of sun and protection is only needed during the hottest part of summer days. It requires a lot of water and the soil in the pot should be kept moist. To provide sufficient nourishment liquid manure should be given weekly. One teaspoon of liquid manure diluted in 2 pints of water is sufficient for about twenty plants.

Sinningia (Gloxinia)

181   Only botanists call this plant Sinningia, lay people still use the name Gloxinia for this profuse-flowering house plant. It can be kept for years as the tuber will overwinter. It comes in many beautiful colours and the red and blue varieties especially are very attractive.

Early in the summer florists have the plant in full bloom and it is very tempting to buy one. However, it is better to take one with many buds and a few open flowers so that you can enjoy it much longer. Gloxinia must have a light position but it needs protection against strong sunlight. The florist will supply the plant in a good potting compost, but if you wish it to flower for a long time, some additional nourishment is needed. This can be supplied by a small weekly dose of diluted liquid manure. Keep the soil in the pot moist and as long as it is not in flower, regular spraying is beneficial.

After flowering the plant should be allowed to die down and it should no longer be watered nor given liquid manure. When the leaves have all withered, the pot can be put away in a cupboard and you can forget it during winter. Early in the spring, you should remove the old tuber from the soil, replace the dry, stale soil with fresh potting compost and repot the plant. Place the pot in a warm room. As soon as the new shoots are about 3 inches high, protection against direct sunlight is necessary.

Skimmia japonica

182   Skimmia is really a hardy, evergreen, berry-bearing garden shrub. Cultivated as a house plant, it can only be a temporary visitor. In a normally heated room the temperature is too high and the atmosphere too dry. Better results are achieved in a moderately heated room, but the plant thrives best in an unheated but frost-free place. The flowers are insignificant and the berries are the main attraction. Some species only produce male or female flowers, but if you order Skimmia japonica you can rely on it to produce berries. If you plant other Skimmias in the garden, you must get a male plant as well, although it does not produce berries, which is essential for cross pollination. If you do not do this, the female plant will be unable to produce berries. The shrub requires a light and sunny position and keep the soil in the pot moist. No spraying is required in a cool environment, but when it becomes warm, the leaves should be moistened daily. After the red berries drop, the plant can be put in the open ground, allowing it plenty of space. It will not do well in limy soil, so acid or peat is essential. You should fill the hole in which you wish to plant it with a mixture of peat-moss, rotted cow manure and sharp sand. During the winter in cold gardens this shrub should be covered with a few green spruce branches for protection.

Solanum capsicastrum (Winter cherry)

183 This well-known and popular house plant is a native of Brazil and looks very effective in late autumn and winter when it is smothered with little miniature orange-like fruits. The smell of the green leaves is not pleasant. It is a robust indoor plant and does not require much warmth. A normally heated room is too warm. The fruit last longest if the plant is kept in an unheated frost-free room. Water with tepid water in such a cool environment. The best time to buy this plant is the autumn when they are readily available. The soil in the pot should be kept moist and a weekly dose of diluted liquid manure is beneficial.

When the fruits shrivel up and drop in the early spring, you should take the plant out of its pot, remove all the old soil from the roots and repot in fresh potting compost. If pruning is necessary, now is the time. Place the plant in a cool but sunny position. After mid-May the plant can be plunged in the garden, in its pot, preferably in a sunny spot. Do not forget to water it. In mid-October bring the plant back into the house. The plant can be propagated by cuttings. Young shoots can be placed in a jam jar filled with water in early spring. When there are sufficient roots, the young plants may be potted.

The plant can also be grown from seed and sowing should take place in early spring. Keep the pot in a warm room. When the seeds have germinated, the seedlings must be pricked out and later on be potted up.

Sparmannia africana (African Hemp)

184   This plant needs plenty of space as it may develop into quite a bushy plant. However, by the time an old plant becomes as large as this, you will have sufficient young plants from cuttings to replace the old one. Sparmannia is a plant which does flower, although people are not always successful in making it. This is because one forgets that the plant needs a resting period. Immediately after flowering, which is in May or June, the plant needs a rest, so stop watering and giving it manure. All the large green leaves will drop, which is just what we want. A month later the plant can be cut back severely, the spent soil among the roots should be removed and replaced by fresh potting compost. You may plunge the plant in its pot in the garden during the summer, but it can also remain indoors. A great deal of watering is necessary, and when it is growing vigorously after repotting, a weekly dose of diluted liquid manure is essential.
Do not keep Sparmannia in a warm place during the winter. The temperature of the living-room is too high and the atmosphere too dry which causes the leaves to turn yellow. It thrives much better in a very moderately heated room. Very large plants will have to be removed to the gardenroom where you can place them in a tub. Although it tolerates a good deal of sun, some protection is needed in the summer during the hottest part of the day.

Spathiphyllum

185   The form of its growth indicates that this plant belongs to the Arum group. The colour of the bract or spathe as it is called is grey-white with a touch of lilac and it is extremely beautiful. The leaves are shiny green, and the plant is very attractive, even when not in flower. However, flowering continues right through the summer and even in the early spring and late autumn it may produce some flowers.

Spathiphyllum should be kept in a normally heated room and in a very moist atmosphere, so frequent spraying with tepid water is essential. Never use cold water straight from the tap, as this is most damaging to the plant. The plant tolerates a good deal of sunshine but it needs some shading during the early spring and summer.

Propagation by dividing the plant can only be done in early spring. Remove the large plant from its pot and divide into several sections. Each section can be grown separately. A good-sized plant can be divided into three. You must provide it with a good potting compost and as a well-aerated soil mixture is appreciated, mix some peat moss with the compost. Its requirement for water is reduced during the winter, but the plant does not have a real resting period. Do not forget the crocks at the bottom of the pot when repotting. The plant is very susceptible to spent soil, so repot frequently.

Stenotaphrum secundatum (americanum) (Variegated grass)

186   This variegated grass is still quite popular as an ornamental foliage plant. In its green variety, it has little interest to the eye, but the variegated form is well worth growing. It is frequently seen naturalized in Southern Europe, especially in Spain, Portugal and also in the Canary Islands, where it is used in lawns.

Grown as a house plant, it does not require a high temperature and will do well in a moderately heated room. During the summer it can be plunged in its pot in the garden. Do not forget to water it. When indoors the plant needs full sunlight, as if it is placed in a dark position the leaves will become entirely green; when green leaves appear, they should be removed.

The plant forms many shoots which makes propagation easy. Often these shoots have developed with roots, which will make the job even easier, as the shoots can be placed straight into a pot. This may be done during the spring, summer or autumn. Place a few shoots together in a normal sized pot and you will soon have a bushy plant. Watering in a cool room in the winter should be done with tepid water. There is no resting period and the plant should be watered freely even during wintertime. A weekly dose of diluted liquid manure is beneficial.

Stephanotis floribunda (Clustered Wax-flower, Madagascar Jasmine)

187 Stephanotis is a twining shrub which should preferably be grown in the open soil of a hothouse. Nowadays good results have been achieved with it as a house plant, especially in centrally heated rooms, where the temperature remains even and where the plant will grow successfully so long as the atmosphere is humid enough. Young plants do not flower very well for the first few years, but as they grow older, they improve. The fragrant white flowers, so well-known in bridal bouquets, are well worth extra care and attention. During the first years no support is required, but after that a wire is needed. The shoots can be twined around it, thus reducing the space it requires. The plant demands a very moist atmosphere and the leaves have to be moistened daily. Use tepid water since cold water straight from the tap is very harmful. The plant is best grown with the so-called deep-dish method. A saucer is lowered upside down into a deep dish containing water in such a way that the bottom of the saucer is just above the water level. A plant placed on this is just above the water but not in it. It should flower from early summer to autumn. Watering must be reduced during winter and any old or dead shoots can be removed in the spring. It needs plenty of sun during the winter, but protection from strong sunlight is needed in the summer. Give it a weekly dose of diluted liquid manure during the growing period. The plant can be propagated in the early spring from cuttings.

Strelitzia reginae (Bird of Paradise Flower)

188 This is a very well-known and exotic plant. It is often sold as a cut flower and used in floral arrangements. It is a native of South Africa and frequently growns in the Canary islands. Grown as a house plant it needs plenty of space, and it does very well in a conservatory or small greenhouse. It may not be easy to obtain a plant of it as only few nurseryman stock them. In Holland there are large hothouses full of it where it is usually cultivated in the open soil of the hothouse. If grown as a house plant, you will probably start off with a pot plant which will soon have to be repotted into a very large pot. Use the normal potting compost, mixed with a little heavy loam (which has been subjected to frost to make it crumble easily) and rotted manure. This plant needs an enormous amount of nourishment and so weekly manuring is essential. The room temperature need not be very high, a moderately heated room being sufficient. It may go on flowering for the best part of the year, depending on its position and the treatment it gets. The plant will eventually outgrow its large pot and will then have to be transplanted into a tub. This must be done very carefully, as the roots are easily damaged. Provide good drainage by a generous layer of broken crocks. The plant needs protection against strong sunlight.

Streptocarpus (Cape Primrose)

189 Nowadays Streptocarpus are grown as house plants and with great success, I am pleased to say. They occur in many shades of blue and pink and white and all the intermediate colours. You will have noticed a resemblance to the Gloxinia, but this plant has no tuber and therefore cannot overwinter in dry soil. Nevertheless, the plant will last for years and can be kept during the winter in a moderately heated room. It should not have much water during that period and manuring should cease altogether. Repot in early spring, shaking the old soil off the roots, and replace it with fresh potting compost. Streptocarpus does not have deep roots and it therefore prefers a shallow pot. Do not forget the crocks at the bottom of the pot. If you use pots of the normal depth one third of them must be filled with crocks. Peat moss should be mixed with potting compost, as the plant likes a nutritious, well-aerated soil mixture. Shading from strong sunlight after mid-April is essential. The first flower buds will develop in the spring. Give the plant a weekly dose of diluted liquid manure and keep the soil damp. Propagate by leaf cuttings, which are made by cutting large leaves into small pieces and placing them in a small pot filled with soil.

Syngonium

190 This is a very decorative climbing shrub which resembles a Philodendron. A very moist atmosphere is essential for it which makes cultivation with the so-called deep-dish method desirable. Lower a saucer upside down in the centre of a deep dish containing water until the bottom of the saucer is just above the water level. When the pot is placed on this, the plant will be just above the water but not in it. The humidity around the plant is now very much greater. In addition, the rather large leaves should be sponged daily with tepid water and the soil should be kept damp. The plant can only be grown in a normally heated room and after mid-April until mid-October protection against strong sunlight is necessary.

The stems of the Syngonium may reach to a considerable height but it can easily be cut back and the plant will form more new shoots towards the base. If the plant is doing well, it will produce aerial roots which is a sign that the atmosphere is humid enough. Do not cut off these roots, but if you wish to use the top as a cutting, some of these roots can be included with the cutting and used as normal roots. The plant needs plenty of nourishment and a weekly dose of diluted liquid manure is beneficial. Plants which have been overwintered should be repotted in the spring. Mix some peat-moss with a standard potting compost for it, as the plant likes an aerated soil mixture.

Thea (Camellia) japonica (Camellia)

191   This evergreen plant is much better known as Camellia than by its obsolete name, Thea japonica. It makes a most beautiful house plant, but requires careful treatment. There are many complaints about its dropping its flowers but this can be prevented if the plant is left in peace. Constant change of position harms the plant, and if the plant has to be moved, you should make a mark on the pot so that it is replaced in exactly the same position. Camellias thrive on a window sill facing East as the differences in temperature are not so great there. No protection from the sun is needed in such a site but the plant does need shading on a sill facing South. The dropping of flower buds can also be prevented by ceasing to give it liquid manure as soon as the buds start to form. Liquid manure is very beneficial but it should not be given just before or just after flowering. Frequent spraying is good for the plant, especially when the buds become large. The plant can then be sprayed a few times daily with tepid water.

Camellias do not require much warmth. A very moderately heated room is sufficient for them during the winter, and after mid-May plants can be plunged in the garden in their pots, in a slightly shaded position. If the plant has grown too much after flowering, it may be cut back, which can be done at the same time as repotting. Mix some sandy peat with the potting compost. There are many different colours, but a double pink variety is particularly beautiful.

Thunbergia alata (Black-eyed Susan)

192 This plant is sometimes known as Black-eyed Susan which is descriptive of it. It is an annual climber which you can raise from seed. Sow it early in spring in a pot indoors, filling a pot with finely sieved soil and covering the seeds lightly. Place a piece of glass and paper on top of the pot. When the seeds have germinated, both glass and paper have to be removed.

Thunbergia can be grown as a bushy plant if a few plants are placed in a wide pot. They will develop quite rapidly in a warm and sunny room and soon need support. You can either place some thin stakes in the pot, or shape a wire into a hoop, round which the long trailers can easily be trained. One variety has lovely orange flowers with a black 'eye' but there are also yellow or white varieties with black centres, as well as doubles.

Thunbergia requires a lot of sun and only at the height of summer some protection is needed against strong sunlight. In such a sunny position it needs plenty of water and it may be necessary to do this more than once a day. A weekly dose of liquid manure is beneficial. Flowering is less usual in winter and the plant may lose some leaves, however, if treated well, it may survive. If the atmosphere is dry, daily spraying is necessary.

Tillandsia lindeniana (Blue Bromelia)

193   This Blue Bromelia is an extremely handsome plant and flowers over a long period as flowers are constantly developing. When flowering ceases, you may be very disappointed, as this particular plant will never flower again. The only thing to do is to grow on the young shoots, which have formed in the meantime at the base of the mother plant. When they are approximately 4 to 6 inches high, they can be detached with their roots and grown separately. The root system is not very highly developed and the pot need only be relatively small. When potting up the young plant, give it a generous layer of crocks in the bottom of the pot. You need a special soil mixture of peat-moss, Osmunda fibre, decomposed leaf-mould and some rotted cow manure. Although a light position is essential, the plant must be protected against strong sunlight. Regular spraying is beneficial but tepid water must be used. The plant grows well in a normally heated room. A weekly dose of diluted liquid manure should be given although the soil mixture is already rich. This Bromelia can also be grown on a dead tree trunk. You should first tie a wad of moss and earth to the trunk, with some of the same mixture as the soil in the pot. Billbergia nutans is a somewhat similar plant which is sometimes called the nodding Bromelia. It needs less warmth and can be propagated by division, which is much easier. You may do this immediately after flowering.

Tradescantia (Wandering Jew)

194 These well-known plants are found in many houses. They originally came from Central America and are named after John Tradescant, gardener to Charles I. The leaves of the different varieties are small, oval and pointed, variegated white or cream with yellow stripes, sometimes pale red. They grow rapidly and are vigorous plants which can be propagated easily from cuttings. This can be done right throughout the year. When a plant gets old and devoid of leaves or has straggly growth, the time has come to take cuttings. Take about 7 young shoots approximately 3 inches long and place them in a normal sized pot; very soon you will have a bushy plant. The variety with plain green leaves grows rapidly and new cuttings will have to be made every three months or so. The other varieties grow less quickly. If any green shoots occur on variegated varieties they should be removed at once, as they will soon get the upper hand. Tradescantias can flower, but the real attraction of the plant is in the leaves. It makes very little demands as regards cultivation and can be grown in a very moderately heated room. They can stand a good deal of sunlight but need some protection during the hottest part of the day. They may be used as a hanging plant and also look quite attractive in plant troughs. They can be watered freely and a small dose of diluted liquid manure is beneficial. Tradescantias are not often repotted, it is better to make new plants from cuttings.

Tulipa (Tulips)

195   To bring the tulips on to flower early is a fascinating job which many housewives undertake, since tulips can be forced with great success. Order the bulbs towards the end of August from a reliable firm. There are numerous varieties and colours, double and single ones, early and late. If you wish them to flower early, order the early varieties; some early and extra early varieties are really excellent. Place a layer of ordinary garden soil in the bottom of the bowl, without any additional compost. Put the bulbs on this in such a way that they support one another. Fill the bowl with garden soil so that the tips of the bulbs are just below the surface. The pots can now be plunged in the garden, preferably in a shady place, some 4 inches below the level of the ground, in a position where they will not be troubled by surface water. Wait until the tips have grown about 3 inches high when the pots are ready to be romoved to the warm livingroom in full daylight. If you have no garden, you can put the pots in a cellar or dark cupboard, but the soil must be kept moist. When taken into a warm room the soil must also be kept moist. After flowering the bulbs are worthless and can be thrown away, as they are no longer suitable for early cultivation, or for planting in the garden.

Vallota speciosa (Scarborough Lily)

196 Your first glance will tell you that this is a miniature form of the Amaryllis or Hippeastrum. Although much smaller in size, the red flowers are no less beautiful, and it is not surprising that these bulbs are so popular for indoor cultivation. The bulbs should be ordered in February from a reliable dealer. They like company and three planted together in one wide pot will do better than one bulb in an individual pot. Do not forget that Vallota needs a very nutritious soil. Use good potting compost mixed with a little cow manure. Vallota needs very little heat and can be made to flower beautifully in a slightly heated room. After potting the bulbs you should water them sparingly at first, until the lily-like leaves appear. Watering can be increased and soon the flower will open. Only after flowering should liquid manure be given in small weekly diluted dose until the rest period starts in mid-October. From then onwards manuring should cease and watering can be greatly reduced if the plant is in a cool position. In the early spring the bulbs can be taken from the pot and the old and dry earth removed. Plant again in fresh potting compost. The plant needs protection against strong sunlight during the summer months.

Vinca rosea (Catharanthus roseus-Madagascar Periwinkle)

197   Vinca rosea is not a very well-known plant. Another species of the same family is Vinca major the hardy Periwinkle which is frequently grown in gardens. There is a variety of this latter with white flowers, but Vinca rosea is more beautiful. However, Vinca rosea can only be cultivated indoors. It requires a humid atmosphere which means it should be sprayed frequently with tepid water. It likes a lot of water and the soil in the pot should be kept moist.

Propagation by means of cuttings is fairly easy. This may be done in early spring or early summer; young shoots approximately 3 inches long will root easily in a small pot filled with sandy soil. In order to get a well established bushy plant it is necessary to nip the tops out of the young plants. Place the Vinca in a sunny position but give it some shade during the hottest part of the day during the summer. Do not leave young plants too long in a small pot as they will soon need a bigger one. Use good potting compost mixed with a little rotted cow manure, as the plants need a very nutritious soil.

Prune early, since the plant will have lost some leaves during the winter and may look a little bare. Repotting can be done simultaneously. Shake the old soil from the roots and replace it by fresh potting compost.

Vriesea splendens (Bromelia)

198   This Bromeliad is sometimes known as Vriesea speciosa major, but the florist usually knows it as Vriesea splendens. It is so named because of the splendid red flowers which it produces. Even when not in flower the plant is attractive, the leaves are dark brown with distinct dark green bands.

Nearly all Bromeliads should be grown in a normally heated room with a moist atmosphere. Frequent spraying is necessary but this should only be done with tepid water. The soil in the pot should be kept moist.

This Bromeliad only flowers once from the same plant. This is a pity really, but at about the time that flowering commences, several young shoots will have formed at the base. When these are about 6 inches long, they can be removed complete with roots from the mother plant and grown on individually. Normal potting compost should not be used for it; you need a mixture of chopped peat-moss and decomposed leaf-mould, and some decomposed spruce needles may be added. Do not forget the broken crocks in the bottom of the pot. The plant needs protection against too strong sunlight. In addition to this nutritious soil mixture, the plant also needs a weekly dose of diluted liquid manure. Once the flower has emerged from the centre of the rosette you should no longer pour water down the leaf tubes, although this is appreciated by the plant before the flower appears. If you do this, then replace the water once a week.

Zantedeschia aethiopica (Arum or Calla Lily)

199   This is a very well-known, profusely flowering plant. It used not to be acceptable as a cut flower for decorative purposes because of its frequent use as a funeral flower. However, as an indoor plant the Arum is very popular. There are often complaints that it does not flower. This is probably because people forget to give the plant a resting period. This should be at the end of May and last for a month. Do not give any manure, cease watering and allow the green leaves to die off. Remove the plant from the pot towards the end of June. Cut the dead leaves away and shake the old and dry soil from the roots. Place the plant in the open ground of the garden in such a position that it has a little shade during the hottest part of the day. Fill the hole for the roots with good potting compost and water freely. If you have no garden, repot the plant in fresh potting compost and water freely.

At the end of September remove the plant from the garden with a good lump of earth around the roots and plant it in a big pot. In mid-October move the plant indoors. At first it should be placed in an unheated room, but when the temperature drops the plant should be removed to the living-room, and watered freely as the plant likes a humid atmosphere. It grows enormously and needs a lot of nourishment, hence the weekly dose of diluted liquid manure. Propagate by dividing the plant after the rest period.

Zygocactus truncatus (Crab cactus)

200   This winter flowering cactus is known as the Crab cactus. It flowers profusely. Plants which have been grafted onto other cacti flower much better than plants which have been grown from cuttings. There are many complaints about failures, mainly about the sudden shedding of flower buds and open flowers. This can be prevented if you leave the plant alone as much as possible from mid-October onwards. Stop giving it liquid manure and reduce watering. It really needs a rest while the formation of the flower buds goes on. When you see these developing at the ends of the leaves, then watering can be increased slightly and more water be given when the buds swell. After flowering the plant needs another six weeks rest, when it can be repotted. Use a good potting compost, as cactus soil is not suitable.

Bud and flower shedding can also be avoided by keeping the plant in exactly the same position, so place a mark on the front of the pot to enable you to replace the pot the same way. Propagation by cuttings is not difficult and can be done immediately after flowering. Young leaves will root easily in a small pot filled with sandy soil. The Crab cactus may be plunged in the soil in its pot during the summer; put the pot in a shady position and take it back indoors at the beginning of October.

Index

The numbers in this index do not refer to the pages, but to the pictures of the plants.

Abutilon (Flowering maple) 1
Acacia armata (Kangeroo thorn) 2
Acalypha hispida (Red-hot cat's tail, Chenille plant) 3
Achimenes 4
Achyranthes verschaffeltii (Iresine herbstii) 115
Adiantum (Maidenhair fern) 5
Aechmea fasciata (Bromeliad) 6
Aechmea fulgens (Bromeliad) 7
African violet 169
Afternoon flower 120
Agave americana 8
Aglaonema 9
Allamanda cathartica 10
Aloe arborescens (Tree aloe) 11
Aloe, partridge-breasted 12
Aloe, tree 11
Aloe variegata (Partridge-breasted aloe) 12
Amaryllis (Hippeastrum Hybrid) 106
Amazon lily 82
Ampelopsis brevipedunculata elegans 13
Ananas comosus (Pineapple) 14
Anthurium andreanum (Lakanthurium) 15
Anthurium crystallinum 16
Anthurium scherzerianum (Flamingo flower) 17
Aphelandra squarrosa Leopoldii 18
Aralia (False) 72
Aralia (Fatsia Japonica) 90
Aralia, Japanese 90
Araucaria heterophylla (Norfolk Island Pine) 19
Ardisa crispa 20
Aregelia (Neoregelia - Bromelia) 21
Aregelia carolinae 21
Arum 185
Arum (Spathiphyllum) 185
Arum (Zantedeschia aethiopica) 199
Asparagus fern 22
Asparagus sprengeri (Asparagus) 23
Aspidistra lurida 24
Asplenium nidus (Bird's nest fern) 25

Astrophytum myriostigma (Bishop's Mitre) 26
Aucuba japonica variegata (Spotted or Variegated Laurel) 27
Azalea, indoor (Rhododendron simsii) 164
Azalea, Japanese (Rhododendron obtusum) 163
Azalea, obtusa 163
Azalea, simsii 164
Balsam 113
Bead plant 131
Begonia corallina 28
Begonia Gloire de Lorraine 29
Begonia metallica 30
Begonia rex 31
Begonia semperflorens 32
Begonia tuberous-rooted hybrids 33
Begonia, winter-flowering 29
Beloperone guttata (Shrimp plant) 34
Bird of paradise flower 188
Bird's nest fern 25
Bishop's mitre 26
Black-eyed Susan 192
Bougainvillea glabra var. sanderiana 35
Bromelia blue 193
Bromelia (Aechmea-Aregelia-Cryptanthus-Guzmania-Vriesea) . . 6, 7, 21, 66, 101, 198
Broom 69
Browallia 36
Brunfelsia (Franciscea) 37
Busy Lizzy 113
Cabbage tree, New Zealand 60
Cactus, gherkin 47
Cactus, leaf 138
Cactus, oldman 44
Cactus, opuntia 134
Cactus, Peireskia godseffiana 138
Caladium 38
Calathea makoyana (Maranta, Peacock plant) 39
Calceolaria (Slipper flower, Slipper-wort) 40
Calla lily 199
Callisia elegans (Tradescantia) 41
Camellia 191
Campanula isophylla alba 42
Canna lucifer (Indian flowering reed) 43
Cape jasmine 98
Cape leadwort 153
Cape primrose 189
Capsicum (Solanum capsicastrum - Winter Cherry) 183
Cephalocereus senilis (Old Man Cactus) 44
Cereus peruvianus 45
Ceropegia linearis (Chinese Lantern plant) 46
Chamaecereus silvestrii (Gherkin Cactus) 47

Chamaedorea (Palm) 48
Chenille plant 3
Cherry, winter 183
China, rose of 105
Chinese lantern plant (Ceropegia linearis) 46
Chinese primula (Primula sinensis) 157
Chlorophytum comosum (Spider plant) 49
Christmas pride 168
Christmas rose 104
Cineraria 179
Cissus antarctica (Kangaroo Vine) 50
Citrus japonica (Miniature Orange tree) 51
Clerodendrum thomsonae (or var. balfouri) 52
Cleyera japonica (Eurya Japonica) 53
Cliff brake fern 142
Climbing figleaf palm 89
Climbing lily 99
Clivia 54
Coconut palm 55
Cocos (Syagrus) weddeliana (Palm) 55
Codiaeum (Croton) 56
Coleus 57
Columnea 58
Convallaria majalis (Lily of the Valley) 59
Cordyline (New Zealand Cabbage tree) 60
Corytholoma (Gesneria) 61
Crassula falcata 62
Crassula lycopodioides (Shoe-lace plant) 63
Creeping fig 94
Crocus 64
Crossandra infundibuliformis 65
Croton (Codiaeum) 56
Crown of Thorns 86
Cryptanthus (Earth Star) 66
Cyclamen persicum (Sowbread) 67
Cyperus alternifolius (Umbrella plant) 68
Cyrtodeira reptans (Episcia reptans) 80
Cyrtomium falcatum (Polystichum falcatum) 155
Cytisus racemosus (Broom) 69
Dieffenbachia (Dumb Cane) 70
Dipladenia 71
Dizygotheca elegantissima (False Aralia) 72
Dracaena fragrans 73
Dracaena godseffiana 74
Dracaena sanderiana 75
Dumb cane 70
Earth star 66
Echeveria metallica 76
Echeveria setosa 77

Echinocactus grusonii (Golden Ball) 78
Echinopsis multiplex 79
Epiphyllum (Phyllocactus ackermannii) 149
Episcia dianthiflora 80
Episcia reptans (Cyrtodeira reptans) 80
Erica gracilis (Heath) 81
Erica wilmorei 81
Eucharis grandiflora (Amazon Lily) 82
Euonymus japonicus 83
Euonymus radicans var. fortunei 84
Euphorbia fulgens (Spurge) 85
Euphorbia milii Crown of Thorns 86
Euphorbia pulcherrima (Poinsettia) 87
Eurya japonica (Cleyera Japonica) 53
Exacum affine 88
Fatshedera (Climbing figleaf palm) 89
Fatsia japonica (Figleaf palm or Japanese Aralia) 90
Fern 129
   Asparagus 22
   Bird's nest 25
   Blue 154
   Cliff brake 142
   Maidenhair 5
   Stag's horn 152
Ficus diversifolia 91
Ficus elastica var. decora (Rubber Plant) 92
Ficus lyrata (Fiddle-leaved Fig) 93
Ficus pumila (Creeping Fig) 94
Fig, creeping 94
   Fiddle-leaved 93
Figleaf palm 90
Fittonia 95
Flamingo flower (Anthurium scherzerianum) 17
Flowering maple 1
Fragaria indica (Strawberry) 96
Franciscea (Brunfelsia) 37
Fuchsia 97
Gardenia jasminoides (Cape Jasmine) 98
Geranium (Pelargonium grandiflorum) 139
Geranium (Pelargonium zonale) 140
Geranium (Pelargonium zonale Black Vesuvius) 141
Gesneria (Corytholoma) 61
Gloriosa (Climbing Lily) 99
Gloxinia 181
Golden ball 78
Grape ivy (Rhoicussus rhombifolia) 166
Grass, variegated 186
Grevillea robusta (Silky Oak) 100
Guzmania (Bromelia) 101

Gynura aurantiaca	102
Heath	81
Hedera helix (Ivy)	103
Hellebore	104
Helleborus hybrids (Hellebore, Christmas Rose)	104
Helleborus niger	104
Hemp, african	184
Bowstring or Angola	171
Hibiscus rosa sinensis (Rose of China)	105
Hippeastrum hybrid (Amaryllis)	106
Hortensia (Hydrangea)	110
Hoya bella (Small Wax-flower)	107
Hoya carnosa (Wax-flower)	108
Hyacinth	109
Hydrangea (Hortensia)	110
Hypocyrta strigillosa	111
Hypoestes sanguinolenta	112
Impatiens (Busy Lizzy, Balsam)	113
Indian flowering reed (Canna lucifer)	43
Ipomoea (Morning Glory)	114
Iresine herbstii (Achyranthes verschaffeltii)	115
Iris reticulata	116
Ivy	103
Ivy, grape	166
Ixora	117
Japanese azalea (Rhododendron obtusum, Azalea obtusa)	163
Japanse aralia	90
Jasmine	118
Jasmine, cape	98
Madagascar	187
Jasminum (Jasmine, Jessamine)	118
Jessamine	118
Kalanchoe	119
Kangaroo thorn	2
Kangaroo vine	50
Lakanthurium	15
Lampranthus blandus (Afternoon flower)	120
Lantana camara	121
Laurel, spotted or variegated	27
Leadwort, cape	153
Leaf cactus (Pereskia godseffiana)	138
Lily, amazon	82
Lily, climbing	99
Lily of the valley	59
Lily, Scarborough	196
Lithops (Pebble plants)	122
Madagascar jasmine	187
Madagascar periwinkle	197
Maidenhair fern	5

Mammillaria	123
Maple, flowering	1
Maranta (Calathea makoyana)	39
Maranta leuconeura var. kerchoveana (Ten Commandment plant)	124
Maranta tricolor	124
Medinilla magnifica	125
Miltonia (Pansy-orchid)	126
Monstera deliciosa (Swiss Cheese plant)	127
Morning glory	114
Moss, tropical	178
Mother-in-law's tongue	172
Mother of thousands	174
Narcissus	128
Neoregelia-Bromelia (Aregelia)	39
Nephrolepis (Fern)	129
Nerium oleander (Oleander)	130
Nertera granadensis (depressa) (Bead plant)	131
Norfolk Island pine (Araucaria heterophylla)	19
Notocactus leninghausii	132
Oak, silky	100
Odontoglossum grande (Orchid)	133
Oleander (Nerium oleander)	130
Opuntia	134
Opuntia ficus-indica	134
Orange tree, miniature	51
Orchid (Miltonia - Odontoglossum - Paphiopedilum)	126, 133, 136
Palm, climbing figleaf	89
Coconut	55
Figleaf	90
Pandanus veitchii (Screw Pine)	135
Pansy-orchid	126
Paperwhites (Narcissus)	128
Paphiopedilum (Venus Slipper)	136
Passiflora caerulea (Passion flower)	137
Passion Flower	137
Peacock plant	39
Pebble plants	122
Pedlar's basket	174
Pelargonium grandiflorum	139
Pelargonium zonale (Geranium)	140
Pelargonium zonale Black Vesuvius	141
Pellaea rotundifolia (Cliff brake fern)	142
Pellionia pulchra	143
Peperomia caperata	144
Peperomia marmorata	145
Pereskia godseffiana (Leaf cactus)	138
Periwinkle, Madagascar	197
Pernettya mucronata	146
Philodendron panduriforme	147

Philodendron wendlandii	148
Phyllocactus ackermannii (Epiphyllum)	149
Pilea cadierei	150
Pilea spruceana	151
Pine, Norfolk Island	19
Screw	135
Pineapple	14
Platycerium bifurcatum (Stag's Horn fern)	152
Plumbago capensis (Cape leadwort)	153
Poinsettia	87
Polypodium crispum glaucum (Polypody or Blue fern)	154
Polypody	154
Polystichum falcatum (Cyrtomium Falcatum)	155
Pomegranate	160
Primrose, cape	189
Primula, chinese	157
Primula malacoides	156
Primula obconica	156
Primula sinensis (Chinese Primula)	157
Pteris cretica	158
Pteris tremula	159
Punica granatum (Pomegranate)	160
Purple heart	180
Pyrrheimia loddigesii (Tradescantia fuscata)	161
Red-hot cat's tail	3
Rhipsalidopsis gaertneri (Schlumbergera gaertneri)	162
Rhododendron obtusum (Azalea obtusa, Japanese Azalea)	163
Rhododendron simsii (Azalea simsii, Indoor Azalea)	164
Rhoeo spathacea	165
Rhoicissus rhombifolia (Grape Ivy)	166
Rochea coccinea	167
Rose, Christmas	104
Rose of China	105
Rubber plant (Ficus elastica var. decora)	92
Ruellia devosiana (Christmas Pride)	168
Saintpaulia ionantha (African Violet)	169
Sanchezia nobilis	170
Sansevieria hahnii (Bowstring hemp, Angola hemp)	171
Sansevieria trifasciata (Mother-in-law's tongue)	172
Saxifraga cotyledon	173
Saxifraga stolonifera var. tricolor (Mother of thousands, Pedlar's Basket)	174
Scarborough lily	196
Schefflera	175
Schlumbergera gaertneri (Rhipsalidopsis)	162
Scindapsus aureus	176
Screw pine	135
Sedum sieboldii	177
Selaginella (Tropical Moss)	178
Senecio (Cineraria)	179

Setcreasea purpurea (Purple Heart) 180
Shoe-lace plant 63
Shrimp plant 34
Silky oak 100
Sinningia (Gloxinia) 181
Skimmia japonica 182
Slipper-flower, slipper-wort 40
Solanum capsicastrum (Winter Cherry) 183
Sowbread 67
Sparmannia africana (African Hemp) 184
Spathiphyllum 185
Spider plant 49
Spleenwort 25
Spurge 85
Stag's horn fern 152
Stenotaphrum secundatum (americanum) (Variegated grass) . . . 186
Stephanotis floribunda (Clustered wax-flower, Madagascan jasmine) . . 187
Strawberry 96
Strelitzia reginae (Bird of Paradise flower) 188
Streptocarpus (Cape Primrose) 189
Swiss cheese plant 127
Syngonium 190
Ten commandment plant 124
Thunbergia alata (Black-eyed Susan) 192
Tillandsia lindeniana (Blue Bromelia) 193
Tradescantia (Callisia elegans) 41
Tradescantia (Wandering Jew) 194
Tradescantia fuscata (Pyrrheimia fuscata) 161
Tropical moss 178
Tulipa (Tulip) 195
Umbrella plant 68
Vallota speciosa (Scarborough Lily) 196
Venus' slipper 136
Vinca rosea (Catharanthus roseus-Madagascar periwinkle) 197
Violet, african 169
Vriesea splendens (Bromelia) 198
Wandering jew 194
Wax flower 108
Wax flower, clustered 187
Wax flower, small 107
Winter cherry 183
Zantedeschia aethiopica (Arum or Calla Lily) 199
Zygocactus truncatus 200

Druk de Lange/van Leer nv-Deventer